THE SEVEN CHURCHES

BEING THE CHURCH
IN A TIME OF CRISIS

MIKE BREEN

The Seven Churches: Being the church in a time of crisis

© Copyright 2020 by Mike Breen

Printed in the United States of America.

Design: Libby Culmer and Jason Zastrow

ISBN: 978-0-9998981-2-3

3DM Publishing

3dmpublishing.com

For Apex

CONTENTS

PREFACE

I have been teaching the material you will find in this book since the 1990s, and I had originally published it in a book back when I lived in Sheffield, England, in that decade .But given the crisis that our world, our families, and our churches find ourselves in after the onset of the worldwide COVID-19 pandemic in 2020, I believe now is the time to reexamine what Jesus says to these seven churches that found themselves in different kinds of crisis.

As we encounter what Jesus says to churches, we will find correction and confidence that helps our churches today continue to faithfully proclaim the name of Jesus in our day. At the end of each chapter, I have included some thoughts and questions that will help us particularly apply the message to each church to our COVID-19 situation and by the shock of lockdown and isolation with most of our churches being closed for public worship. I have already found, and I believe you will too, that the letters John received in his isolation on the Isle of Patmos can empower the church of our day in this time of crisis marked by the isolation of quarantine.

At the end of each chapter, we've added a section called Crisis and Cultural Earthquakes to help you reflect on how the message Jesus shares with the churches may apply to our post-COVID-19 culture..Chapters also have Huddle Study guides with discussion questions designed to help you and your Huddle, house church or missional community to reflect on and discuss what you've read. These questions will help you identify what God is saying and what you should do about it. Often, chapters also have a section for additional reflection that you can use inside or outside of a discipleship group.

I pray God's blessings on you and on your church, and I trust that God will use this book to speak to your church in our day.

INTRODUCTION

Many years ago, when I was a young minister working in the inner city of London, I found that the pace of life and the pressure were starting to show in my home life with my wife and young children, and also at work. Talking it over with my wife Sally, we decided the best thing would be if I took a break and went on a prayer retreat to rest and refocus. Hopefully this time of abiding would allow me to come back to my family and church with fresh vision and vigor. I asked a friend to loan me his camper van for a week, so I could spend time walking and praying in the Black Mountains of South Wales.

During this week, I had a great time walking and talking to the Lord, but quite honestly did not feel as though I had received a fresh vision that I could take back to London with me. It was not that I felt that God was far away — it was just that I was not seeing or hearing anything from him as I prayed and read my bible that I could take back as the tangible product of my retreat.

(I realize now that it was perhaps a mistake to expect a retreat to produce anything, but God answered my prayer anyway - and gave me something which challenged me and changed the way I think forever.)

On my return journey, I stopped in the Forest of Dean, hoping to be able to explore it for a day before returning to London. I arrived late in the afternoon and decided to walk to the local village to buy some supper. By the time I finished eating, the sun was already low in the sky, and evening was arriving. Thinking that the best thing to do was to take a shortcut through the Forest to reach the van before nightfall, I struck out. (It's amazing how foolish some plans sound when you retell them.)

At first I made good progress, but as the evening became night, the Forest became more dense. In some places, it had been planted but not yet thinned out by the Forestry Commission. The trees had grown so close to one another that it was literally impossible to get through. The only path was to find the fire breaks--gaps in the forest cut by the foresters. I finally found a break that seemed to head downhill toward the campsite where I had parked the van. By now it was almost dark, and the first stars had appeared in the sky. Although the fire break was easier to walk through than the rest of the Forest, it had also been left untended and uncleared, and so it was full of undergrowth and fallen trees.

I found myself becoming anxious and alarmed about my predicament. The Forest looked quite dark and foreboding, and the struggle I was having to make it back to the campsite made the situation all the more intimidating. I shot an occasional prayer heavenward, but my main concern was making it out of the Forest as quickly as possible. My focus was on finding safe footings and quick passage. So I was surprised when, unbidden, a vision began to grow first in my mind and then apparently took over my surroundings. It was not so much a mental picture as a sense of stumbling into a scene in which I was now participating.

All around me were cries of battle and scenes of struggle. Two opposing forces engaged in desperate hand-to-hand combat. A combatant whom I immediately knew to be an angel was fighting on behalf of the church, using his sword to beat back his antagonist. The intense struggle was evident in the strain on all the bodies and faces. I could see determination bordering on desperation in the strokes of the angel, whom I now recognized as my champion.   I found myself not only engaged by what I saw, but also personally involved. I shouted encouragement and willed the angel to win. The fight went back and forth, but eventually the angel began to gain the upper hand over his demonic opposition. The dark angel, dressed and protected by his dark armor, stumbled and fell back. My champion, resplendent in armor of light, pressed home the advantage. I was exhilarated and began to inwardly celebrate the fact that the battle would soon be won and the evil spirit would be dealt a final blow. But somehow, the dark angel gained his feet and stood his ground. He was incredibly strong.

As I watched the church's champion continue to fight, hoping to regain the advantage, the demon began to laugh. At first it was a giggle, and then great bellows of laughter as his strength renewed and he stood his ground and began to return the fight to the angel of light. I was furious and wanted so badly for the demon to be routed that I caught myself crying out,"'God, why is he laughing?"

The answer was quiet, certain and assured. "Because he knows the church better than you do. If he gives ground now, he thinks he will be able to take it back again later."

At that point the vision stopped, as though someone had switched off the projector in a cinema. Simultaneously, I stumbled out of the Forest to the verge of the road. I followed the road through the dark back to the van.

Once I was back in the safety of the camper, I examined myself

and discovered that my clothes were streaked with mud and
that my hands and face were cut and scratched. I have never
had another experience like that, but this vision has profoundly
affected the way I understand the work of the church and the
nature of our struggle. The lingering question remains: "How
will God bring about victory through his church against such a
powerful and wily foe?"

THE VISION OF JOHN

The Apostle John knew the answer. His vision, far more profound
than mine, was of the battle and the final victory won by God.
But the agents of that victory were the same people represented
in my vision--the church and the host of angelic forces at God's
disposal. The book of Revelation--the product of John's vision-
-is the triumphant ending of the story of God's struggle against
rebellion and the devil's host. It is the prophecy of the victory
that will be his and ours when Jesus the King returns.

The churches addressed at the beginning of the book of
Revelation were the churches for which John was responsible. He
was their leader and the last of the twelve apostles to survive the
persecution of the church. John received his vision and wrote his
book at the end of his life in the most unlikely of circumstances.
He was on Patmos serving a sentence of enforced labor as
punishment for his determination to stay faithful as a Christian.
By now John was an old man, unsuited to hard physical labor,
but still he rejoiced in the gospel and trusted in the Lord with all
his heart. One Sunday, no doubt following his regime of daily
work in the quarries of Patmos, John was in the Spirit, praying
and meditating. Perhaps he was meditating on the resurrection
of the Lord, since this was the day of the week on which he had
witnessed this resurrection all those years ago. Suddenly, the
scene changed, and John heard a piercing, powerful voice like a
trumpet telling him to send a letter to the churches for which he
was responsible.

John turned and saw that he was surrounded by light emanating from lampstands all around him. Into the scene of light and glory walked an even more glorious vision. Jesus was there. John knew that it was Jesus, but he was dressed in the robes of heaven with the golden sash of kingship tied around his chest. Jesus' hair was now brilliant white, and his eyes, which at first appeared to reflect the light of the candles, were in fact flames themselves. His feet seemed to be glowing red hot, and as he spoke with his voice like a waterfall, it cut John's heart like a sword.

Everything was glory and brilliant shining white, and John could bear the vision no longer. He fell on his face, certain that such a vision would mean his imminent death. But his Lord, now ascended and glorious, was still the Jesus he knew. John felt a hand on his shoulder and heard a familiar voice saying, "Don't be afraid. I am the first and the last. I am the living one, once dead but now alive forever. Death only comes when I say so."

The challenge of my vision in the Forest of Dean has often caused me to ask the question, "Can we win?" This is a vital question, especially for churches in the midst of crisis. John's vision provides the answer. The risen Jesus was equipping the churches of John's time to win. The vision of struggle between good and evil is to encourage Christians in every age with the promise of eventual victory. John's vision begins with the answer and then offers the explanation.

WHAT JESUS WANTS

The answer to my question and the solution to our struggle is that Jesus walks among the lampstands – the churches – personally overseeing and caring for them. The vision of the glorious, ascended, all-powerful Jesus is the answer to all our questions and the promise of ultimate victory. To my question and yours, to John's question and to the question of first century Christians, Jesus says, "Look to me."

When we look to Jesus and concentrate on him, we discover that his voice, like many waters, still washes over us today, and his word like a scalpel-sharp sword cuts away the spiritual diseases and sickness of our lives to bring us life.

Jesus is looking for a healthy church and for effective Christians who allow him to bring new life and health to their spirits. This kind of church and these kinds of Christians will bring the victory that God has planned no matter the crisis. That is why the first phase of John's vision includes an analysis by the risen Lord of the spiritual health of his church and his prescription that will cure its ills.

This analysis and prescription is the subject of this book. I hope that, as the chapters of this book unfold, you will find it possible to apply the teaching of the letters to the churches in Revelation to your own life, but more than that I pray you can apply this teaching , from families on mission, missional communities and house churches through to any gathering of God's people anywhere in the world. The one holy universal church takes many forms Throughout, I have tried to provide ways for each of us to think through and apply the important teaching found in these scriptures.

In these letters--which are so short that we can think of them as postcards from heaven--we have perhaps the clearest insight in the entire Bible as to what Jesus wants from his church. Since this is the one place in the Bible where Jesus himself personally addresses the question, it is worth examining.

THEY WHO HAVE EARS

One of the things you will notice about each of the letters is that each letter concludes with this phrase, "he who has ears, let him hear what the spirit says to the churches." It may seem obvious, but that is supposed to include everyone. It's a universal statement of expectation, because each of us has ears.

Of course the ears that we're speaking about are not defined by physical hearing, but by the capacity each of us has to hear the voice of God. When we are reborn and the spirit of God comes to live within us, this capacity is made real. And so if you have the capacity to hear the voice of God, which is true of all of us, then you need to listen to what the Spirit is saying to the churches. Let all of us who have ears hear what the Spirit is saying to us and to all of the Church.

1

EPHESUS
A CRISIS OF PRIDE

To the angel of the church in Ephesus write:

These are the words of him who holds the seven stars in his right hand and walks among the seven golden lampstands. I know your deeds, your hard work and your perseverance. I know that you cannot tolerate wicked people, that you have tested those who claim to be apostles but are not, and have found them false. You have persevered and have endured hardships for my name, and have not grown weary.

Yet I hold this against you: You have forsaken the love you had at first. Consider how far you have fallen! Repent and do the things you did at first. If you do not repent, I will come to you and remove your lampstand from its place. But you have this in your favor: You hate the practices of the Nicolaitans, which I also hate.

Whoever has ears, let them hear what the Spirit says to the churches. To the one who is victorious, I will give the right to eat from the tree of life, which is in the paradise of God.

Revelation 2:1-7

Several years ago, my family and I were living in Arkansas, but were asked to interview to become the leaders of St. Thomas' Crookes Church in Sheffield, England. We flew across the Atlantic to South Manchester, where Sally's parents lived. After a visit, we set out for Sheffield.

We decided that driving over the Pennines would be the best route there from South Manchester. We loaded the car and set out. Five of us were in the car--Sally, her parents, our son Sam, and me--and I was driving.

A persistent drizzle fell as we made our way through the outskirts of the city. By the time we reached the highway in Stockport, it had become a constant rain. The road climbs from Stockport to Chapel-en-le-Firth, where we planned to turn off and take the Mam Tor road to Castleton. By the time we reached that point, the rain had turned to sleet. I turned to my father-in-law and asked him, "Do you think we might not get through?" He had traveled this road hundreds of times, and his look communicated all I needed to know. But despite his look, I knew we had to get to Sheffield, and I decided to keep going.

Climbing from Chapel-en-le-Frith to Mam Tor takes you to the upper elevation's of the Pennine range. You can be certain that whatever is falling as sleet in Chapel is falling as snow on top. Few other vehicles, aside from the odd Land Rover or off-road vehicle, were on the road. In fact, the only other normal car like ours that we saw actually turned around to go back down the mountain. Snow covered everything. The only way to follow the road was to stay within the verges which were bounded by dry stone walls. Our small front-wheel drive Rover 418 had not enjoyed the greatest record of reliability, but it was doing fine pulling us through what seemed to be an impassable road.

We reached Mam Tor and the top of our climb, and I rather foolishly started to relax, thinking the worst was over. But almost as soon as the car began to descend, I realized I had almost no control over where the car was going. The front-wheel drive did well pulling us uphill, but was of little help on the descent. The car began to slide sideways, as if in slow motion, toward the ditch. All five of us could see what was happening and were struck silent. We were going to tumble down the gully. It was terrifying. The ditch got closer, and I had no control over the car. I tried the brakes, sure they would not help in the least. Then I moaned a vague prayer for help and waited for the inevitable. But incredibly, the tires took hold, and gained sufficient traction to let me accelerate away. At the very last moment, our journey was saved from disaster.

These kinds of experiences tend to help us concentrate our minds. In the moment, fear and determination were the only emotions we could manage. Turning back was no longer an option. The sense of adventure was gone. Even the beauty of the surroundings did not register. We had to hope we could stay on the road and reach the bottom. All eyes were fixed on the road ahead, and no one spoke as we rounded the corner into Winnats Pass.

This Pass is an extremely narrow and steep road from top to bottom. In less than a mile on a single-lane road, you drop from the heights of Man Tor, to the broad, pleasant valley in which Castleton nestles. As we rounded the corner and reached the top of the Pass, we crossed the cattle grid. The sound of the grid on the wheels rattled our jangled nerves further and emphasized the fact that there was only one way to go— down! On a snowbound hillside road, of course, brakes are useless, so I stayed in first gear and crept as slowly as I could through the narrow Pass. We inched our way along the winding road, wondering what would become of us if we slipped again and tumbled into the valley bottom on our left, which was deep enough to swallow many cars our size. The absolute silence in the car only added to the palpable tension. We had a few close calls but gradually, as the bottom came into view, our confidence rose and our tension eased. As we reached the bottom and came out of the deepest snow, we allowed ourselves a little cheer.

We hit snow again on the other side of Hathersage, not far from Fox House, but although this meant a detour, nothing was quite so dangerous as Winnats Pass. When we looked back down the road, we realized we were the last car through. No one else had been so foolhardy as to venture the journey after us.

Having set out an hour earlier than necessary to make the journey, we arrived at our destination an hour late. We were hardly in any state to go into an interview that might change the course of our lives. Later that day, after all the interviewing was over, the chairman of the panel phoned to invite me to become the new Team Rector of St Thomas' Crookes. My rather cautious reply, I think, surprised him. The events of the day had made a strong impression on me. I felt unprepared for any decisions and needed time to process and pray through all that had happened. Later, after talking to Sally, I called back to say that I would come if confirmation from God continued to flow.

By the time the Bishop confirmed the call a week or so later, I was sure that we should leave our home in the United States and travel back to Sheffield for what would almost certainly be a very long time. The reason for this newfound confidence was that God had given me a message for St Thomas' and a vision of what he wanted the church to be. When I returned home, I asked the Lord if he had anything to say or show me about this possible move. I sensed that his reply was that he was sending me and the word he was giving me was Ephesus. This seemed a rather cryptic message, so I decided to study all that I could about Ephesus and pray through what God might be saying. My study proved very fruitful. I not only gained more knowledge, but God gave me insight into what he wanted to do at St Thomas'. I had a chance to share some of this vision with the church before I took up my new post and later, after our arrival, I preached a whole series of sermons which ultimately led to this book. Sometimes one word can go a very long way!

LIFE IN EPHESUS

For its time, Ephesus was a very large and important city. As many as half a million people crowded its streets in the days of Paul. Pergamum, the ancient seat of kings, was the Administrative capital of the region, but Ephesus, holding its strategic position on the west coast of Asia Minor (modern-day Turkey) was the principal city of the region and one of the empire's top five metropolises. Ephesus had perhaps the largest port in the world. All the major trading routes from the east converged there, providing a commercial foundation on which this large and cosmopolitan city was built.

Ephesus was a remarkable city. It was a great center of learning. Students from around the world came to use its libraries, second only to those of Alexandria. It was the principal medical center for the region. Perhaps Luke, the New Testament writer and physician to the Apostle Paul, was trained there. It was also a center for religion and culture. It featured the temple of Diana, one of the seven wonders of the world and at the time the largest single building in the world. The temple contained a black meteorite carved into the shape of a woman's face. This stone was worshiped as the image of Diana, the female deity of the region. The temple was a tremendous attraction in its own right. People from everywhere came to worship and buy their souvenir silver statuettes from one of the gift shops found in the city.

Around AD 51, Paul arrived in Ephesus with his partners in mission, Priscilla and Aquila. It appears that he had been trying to get there for some time, but for one reason or another had been prevented. Luke's account of Paul's progress across Asia Minor indicates that Paul was heading for Ephesus all the time, but the Lord had other plans (Acts 16:6-7). Paul knew that Ephesus was the principal city of the region and understood that the best way to evangelize Asia Minor was to start from this base. When he arrived, he found the city as he expected, ready and prepared for the gospel. The men of the synagogue wanted to hear what Paul had to say. But unusually for Paul, he turned down this opportunity and left Priscilla and Aquila to begin this vital ministry. Paul had to return to Jerusalem to fulfil a vow. It is uncertain why he wanted to do this, but this was perhaps one of the occasions that he specifically asked the Lord to remove his "'thorn in the flesh" when he heard the answer: "My grace is sufficient for you, for my power is made perfect in weakness." (2 Cor. 12:8-9).

After this time in Jerusalem, Paul took a sabbatical in Antioch and then made his way on foot through the whole region, visiting as many of his churches as he was able, eventually reaching Ephesus to spend more than two years there. What he found must have by now become an established ministry. Yet he continued to support himself, like Priscilla and Aquila, by making the tents that he sold to the travelers who passed through the city.

While in Ephesus, Paul taught and trained the local believers in a rented lecture hall which he was probably able to use during the siesta hours in the middle of the day. From there he sent church planting teams into the region to plant churches at Smyrna, Pergamum, Thyatira, Philadelphia, Sardis, Laodicea, and Colossae. One of these teams is mentioned in Colossians, where Paul reminds the Colossian believers that although he himself had never met them, Epaphras, the team leader, had planted the church there on his behalf (Col. 1:7).

In Ephesus Paul saw an incredible explosion of spiritual power. Luke tells us that, in the space of two short years, the whole province of Asia Minor was effectively evangelized and that the extraordinary and miraculous events that occurred in Ephesus led many to receive the gospel and hold the name of the Lord Jesus in high honor (Acts 19:10;17-18). The Ephesian church had become a resource church to the region, sending out missionaries and church planters and offering a teaching and training base that touched all of Asia Minor.

When God said to me the word Ephesus, I believe he was declaring something that had already occurred but it was also something that he desired to develop in the future. The church of St Thomas' was to function as a resource to its city and region. It was to be a base for church planting and mission and a center for teaching and training. Obviously there would be problems and difficulties, but if God was saying this, it would certainly happen. And if you know my story, you know that it did. The 3DM movement of discipleship and mission that has circumnavigated the globe started during my days in Sheffield.

Other parts of the New Testament provided insights about some of the central issues that I needed to face. First and Second Timothy were written to Paul's young friend whom he had sent to lead the church in Ephesus. These letters proved particularly encouraging as I prepared to go back to England. The letters of Ephesians and Colossians, probably both round robin letters read by all Christians in Asia Minor, focused on the supremacy of Christ, the sovereignty of God, and ministry and unity within the body of Christ. These too proved helpful as I reflected on the move. But there was something more--a particular obstacle that the church in Ephesus had faced and that St Thomas' also now faced. In Revelation, seven churches in the region of Asia Minor are addressed. The seven letters begin with Ephesus, the principal church in the principal city. The church was commended for much but was also reprimanded. It had a single, fatal flaw. It had forsaken its first love.

FIRST LOVE
The Ephesian church was praised for its perseverance, hard work, and sound doctrine. They were a biblical church ready to exercise sound judgement, prepared to weigh the ministries and callings

of other leaders according to the light of Scripture. They were adept at spiritual discernment, testing the truth of statements made about and on behalf of God. Today we might identify the Ephesian church with a number of large evangelical churches who have exercised a clear biblical ministry within their cities and regions.

At first glance, Ephesus' report card looked great. They had six or seven As and only one D. The problem was that the D stood for death, because Jesus promised that unless they reclaimed their first love he would remove their lampstand, extinguishing their opportunity to bear witness to the light of Christ. To the Lord, forsaking their first love was no small thing. In fact it was so important that he was prepared to close the church because of it. What a stunning thought! Jesus is prepared to pull the plug on our lampstand if we lose our first love of him.

I am sure that I have wandered carelessly in my walk many times with God and allowed the fires of love to grow dim and my tender relationship with the Lord to grow faint. Thankfully, God has made me aware of these times. Rather than leading me into an experience of cringing condemnation, he has drawn me back to himself. His words of challenge and chastisement have always worked within me for good, and so it was for the church at Ephesus. The last thing that Jesus wanted to do was to close the church and remove its lampstand, but his strong word was calculated to get their attention and draw them back to the love that they had once known.

How did they get into this state? We can really only speculate, but the speculation may be close to the mark if we examine our own experience.

THE PROBLEM OF PRIDE

Ephesus was a successful church, and in my life success has led to pride. That is the crisis this church faced. Let me explain. As a church leader I can say that, when success has arrived, I have been tremendously grateful for all that it brings -- lives changed, new Christians, healing and deliverance, a growing maturity in the people I serve. But before long I have found myself beginning to focus on success and not on the Lord. I have begun to concentrate on what I must do to maintain the success, and not focus on God, the author of the success, and what he wants to do next.

This simple and familiar process opens the door to pride and can lead us within range of the enemy's attack. When God challenges this pattern in our lives, he sometimes uses a painful path of correction. But with the correction comes the open door of forgiveness and the joy of a renewed relationship with him. As soon as we begin to take credit for something that God has done, then we say that the success and blessings we receive are not all of God.

Grace, one of the central teachings of the New Testament, shows us that God initiates, God sustains, and God concludes all that we would consider as good or blessed in our lives. The truth of the gospel is that God sovereignly does it all and invites us to participate with what he is doing. We get to share the celebration and success, but the initiation is all from him. The gospel is all grace and nothing of works. What God has shown me is that when pride creeps in and I begin to congratulate myself for all that I am doing, I lean on my own understanding more and more, trusting in my own strength and hard work. This is a dangerous place, because it draws us away from the Lord and the warmth of his love into the hard grip of human striving.

The effects of pride are varied. As we begin to take credit for the things that God is doing, we also take for granted the good things that we see around us. We compare ourselves with others and see that they do not have the same levels of success, influence, or status. We assume that we have done something to achieve our position, and that they have done something to get stuck in theirs. So subtly, little by little, judgment of others grows within us and our conversations become laced with self-congratulations and criticism of others.

I could offer many stories to illustrate this process from my own experience. One that springs to mind is that of leading an inner-city church in Brixton. After a few years, I was asked to write a book to record the reasons why we were so successful. As I considered these reasons, I somehow missed the message of grace and caught myself thinking that I was the principal reason for all the blessings. This led to an inner unarticulated criticism of other churches in similar situations who were not seeing the growth that we were seeing. God slowly increased the pressure in my own heart, as he withdrew small portions of his grace — programs faltered, services struggled, signs of life diminished — just enough for me to panic! When I realized what was happening, I cried out for forgiveness and mercy. The man who wrote the last chapter was a different one from the man who wrote the first. I was so chastened that my first attempt at the last chapter was rejected by my editor who thought that a ten-page public confession probably was not the way to end the book. Writing the book began as a celebration of self and ended as a recognition of grace.

This process is bad enough in itself, but if you are a leader the consequences can be even more dire. Our conversation and attitudes affect others more because we are looked to for an example. Because of this our pride will be multiplied in the lives of others as they model themselves on us and use our attitudes as an excuse for theirs.

In the time of Paul, the Cayster River on which Ephesus stood was silting up year by year. The authorities tried to dredge it to alter its flow, but the inexorable process continued. Today the ruined remains of Ephesus lie ten miles from the sea. The river estuary on which Ephesus was built choked to death and left the city landlocked and stranded. What is it like to allow the subtle process of pride to grow in our lives? It is like the silting up of a river — invisible at first, but in time we are miles from the sea of God's love and the life of the river no longer flows!

When we begin to take credit for what God is doing, we focus on ourselves and we fail to see Jesus. Because we fail to see Jesus, we fail to see what he has done for us. Our love for him becomes cooler, more distant, and our spiritual life becomes thin and overstretched, and before we know it, we have lost our first love.

It is like the first snow falling on Mam Tor. At first there is no problem for traffic, but in the end Winnats Pass is blocked and traffic can no longer get through. As I was driving the car through those terrible conditions, concerned for the safety of my family and whether we would make it to the interview, somewhere in my heart God was telling me to take notice. Despite the godly ministry of my predecessors, St Thomas' was in danger of forsaking its first love and was at risk of being gripped by the cold process of spiritual decline. This was a hard message for me to share, not least because I was being called to be the next Rector. But when I shared with the church what I heard God saying, there was a general consent to the rightness of what I shared and a wholesale repentance on the part of those who listened. Of course that process of repentance and seeking the Lord for his love and grace continues.

FIRST THINGS FIRST

Do you remember the days when your first love for the Lord flourished? Did it matter what God asked you to do? Did it matter what people thought of you? Was worship wonderful, prayer a joy, and the Bible God's living message to you? The joy of the Lord filled your heart and you cared little for the obstacles and opposition that you faced. Was it a vision of heaven or God's spreading kingdom that gripped your imagination? You were still in the shadow of Calvary, the empty tom, and the day of Pentecost. But what about today? Are the same truths just as central? Is the joy of them still as real?

The experience of first love will be different for each person. But the question remains,'Has our love matured, or have we grown dull and listless and so put ourselves in danger of losing this first love? This question is constantly asked as we read the New Testament. The writer to the Hebrews encourages us to ask the same question and exhorts his readers to return to those early days after they had first received the light (Hebrews 10:32).

The intensity of our first love is something that we must not lose as we grow and mature. It is not to be rejected along with other elements of our early Christian experience which may have arisen from an infantile faith.

ESCAPING PRIDE

Pride will always be the greatest enemy of love, but even with pride there is the means of escape. Peter tells us that God resists the proud and gives grace to the humble (1 Pet. 5:5). Pride has a way of tripping us up because it always comes before a fall. I often find myself feeling foolish because of the way my own pride leads me to stumble in my walk with God. As a theological student, I can remember going to George Carey's church in Durham to listen to David MacInnes. In his sermon he told a wonderful story that seems to illustrate well the problem of pride.

There was an air commodore during the Second World War who went to test a new seaplane that was being developed in the Portsmouth area. The test pilot showed him the new plane and then took the air commodore for a flight around Portsmouth harbor. When they were airborne, the air commodore decided to take the plane through its paces, fly it around, and then land it himself. As he was making his final approach, the test pilot realized with some concern that the air commodore appeared to be bringing the sea plane to land at the local airport. He waited until the very last moment when he was sure that the air commodore had made a terrible mistake. Only then did he turn and say, "Sir, you do realize that this is a seaplane and that we have no wheels to land at the airport?" The air commodore pulled out of his approach just in time and took the plane around to land safely in the harbor. At this point he turned to the test pilot and said, "Of course, I was just testing you and making sure you were fully alert." He opened the door — and stepped straight into the water!

That is what pride does. It trips us up. Pride comes before a fall. At first the fall will be small, but as God's resistance of our proud attitudes continues, and so the falls get greater. The answer is to recognize the fall as an escape. Failure and foolishness become our opportunity to recognize what we are doing and stop. This may be embarrassing. Recognizing fault rarely is anything else but embarrassing. But if we take the opportunity that God provides to recognize our fault and return to him, we will discover again the joy of our first love. On the other hand, if we continue to take ourselves too seriously, being inflated with our own sense of importance, hiding our feelings and constantly pointing to our success, we will lose our first love and grieve the Lord who first loved us and gave himself for us.

THE FRUIT OF PRIDE

Nothing is more dangerous than pride. The Lord will deal with nothing more severely. It strikes at the heart of all our relationships and raises barriers between us and God. If pride lies at the roots of forsaken love, what are its fruits? What does forsaking our first love produce in our lives, and how can we recognize its absence?

Let me tell you a story — an amalgam from several sources — that may help to answer these questions. Stanley and Sue Driver were a success story. Stanley Driver's business was doing very well. He owned a company specializing in surgical equipment. As a job it was both lucrative and interesting work. Stanley's big break came when one of the country's largest medical supply companies asked him to manufacture heart valve catheters at his plant. He had never looked back. He had an established business, a string of patents, and a secure future to look forward to. He had met his wife at university where they were both doing business studies. Both of them had become Christians through the vibrant work of the student Christian Union.

Sue Driver used to do quite a lot for the business in the early days, mainly on the accounts. Now she preferred to focus her energies on the children and the home while maintaining her role as one of the company's directors. She had hoped this would mean she could spend more time getting involved in their church, but she seemed to be busier than ever. She felt as though much of her time was spent running kids from one place to the next: school, parties, gym club, scouts, riding and football. Their children, a boy and a girl, seemed to be growing up happily and doing well at school. Stan and Sue were pleased that all their hard work was paying off.

A few years earlier they had moved to their present house and joined their new church. With the business running well, they could afford a large house in the suburbs, and so they took the opportunity to move from their modest terraced house and to get the children into a better school. Moving of course had its downside. Stan had a longer commute back and forth to work, but their new surroundings, new home, new school and new church seemed to far outweigh anything that they had lost. The small church that they had attended in the city was sorry to see them go. They had both been key figures in the church, serving their time on the church council and as Sunday school teachers. Their intention was to get similarly involved in their new church. At first its size and efficiency discouraged them from offering themselves, and they soon found they quite liked being able to just come along without the added pressure of responsibility.

Success had brought other benefits; their holiday destinations were more exotic, though the amount of time for holidays seemed to be more limited. Of course, they were able to buy nicer things. But over the last few years their quality of life had been affected. Their business often left them tired. New tensions which they had hardly known before began to develop. Stan was much more edgy and more prone to outbursts of anger, and Sue covered up her growing sense of anxiety. She worried about the children. She worried about her husband. She worried about her friends and found herself taking on their worries as well. Occasionally things came to a head and they would realize that life was becoming too intense. To deal with it, they would pack up the car and all go off for the weekend and spend a couple of nights away together, escaping their hectic lifestyle. Of course, this meant that they were not able to go to church, but it seemed the right thing to do.

The shaking began one Sunday in church. As usual, the building was packed with eager and expectant worshippers. The praise and worship had been excellent and the children's work was being run with its usual efficiency. The sound, carefully prepared sermon was being delivered. The Rev. Manley was doing his usual outstanding job. He was a thoughtful and caring pastor who had built this now thriving evangelical church from quite modest beginnings. He was respected by all, sought out as a conference speaker and writer. He was known as one of the country's best preachers, but he was aware that something was lacking from his ministry. Passion for God had marked his early days, but over the years it had ebbed away as he, like his church, had become familiar with success. The process had been at first imperceptible. Dignity replaced devotion. Respectability replaced revival power. Soon the gospel fire was hidden behind the carefully prepared smoke screen of scriptural soundness. Rev. Manley's considerable talents and outward strengths had begun to mask his weaknesses and inner failings.

As he spoke, his powerful style had the congregation hanging on every word. But no one was ready for what came next! He suddenly switched style. Putting aside his notes, he moved away from the lectern and looked intently at his congregation. "You all know that we have been having difficulties finding enough teachers for our children's work, and that recently I've been holding prayer meetings about this growing crisis. But nothing has changed, and I'll be honest, my frustration with you and even the Lord has grown. I've never known a time in this church's history when we have found it so difficult to get things done! We have more people, but our income is no longer growing. We have more to do and fewer people offering to do it. A few days ago, I woke from sleep and something happened that has not happened for a long time. God spoke to me directly! I'd gone to bed as usual, worrying about the church, and had spent most of the night tossing and turning. Eventually I dropped off to sleep and in a dream I saw myself suddenly struck down with a heart attack and being carried by ambulance to the emergency room of our local hospital. I was lying unconscious but was still able to hear the doctor say that he thought my chances were slim. I had a blocked artery and although that could be cleared, he didn't think that my lifestyle would ever become balanced enough to allow me to recover properly. The doctor said, 'His diet is too rich and he does too little exercise!'

"I woke anxious and worried, but realized that the dream meant something. I began to pray and sensed that without a doubt God was speaking to me. I had indulged my theological appetite and had retreated from any active personal witness and spent my whole time writing sermons, doing church work, and spending time with a small group of leaders in the church, all of whom were just like me! Worse still, I had begun to create a church after my own likeness and grow Christians who also indulged their theological tastes and did little with their knowledge other than discuss it. It seemed as though the Lord was saying that my heart was sick and needed help, and that just like me, the church was sick and needed to have its heart healed also.

"Please pray for me and the church as we consider what we must do to rectify this problem. Some of you may feel that this applies to you also. If you would like to meet me privately, please arrange to come and see me when I can talk and pray with you more personally."

Then Rev. Manley walked out! He did not even walk to the door to say goodbye as he normally would. He walked out through the choir door and went to his office!

The congregation sat in stunned silence. Even the organist — usually quick off the mark — was caught out on this occasion, but once he had recovered, he played some appropriate music to cover what was becoming an embarrassing pause in the normally smooth proceedings.

The way home Stan and Sue did not talk very much. Eventually at lunch, Sue said, "Do you think we ought to make an appointment to see Mr. Manley?"

"Why should we do that?" Stan asked, a little too quickly to sound relaxed.

Sue replied, "Because I think our faith is not what it used to be — and anyway it wouldn't do us any harm."

"We may have let things slip a little," Stan said (he had not prayed or read his Bible for months) "but we've been so busy just recently."

"I know we have, that's what I mean. Let's go and see him and see what he has to say." Sue called the church the next day and made an appointment for that week. They were both surprised that they were able to arrange a time so soon. Stan had hoped that he might have more time to start up his quiet times again beforehand.

They arrived at church straight after work. Sue's mother had come round to give the kids their tea. Rev. Manley's secretary showed them through to his office. "Mr. and Mrs. Striver are here," she said as she opened the door.

"That's Driver," Stan said, correcting the obvious error.

"I'm sorry, I must have read the note wrong," said the secretary looking a little embarrassed.

"Come in, come in, take a seat," said Rev. Manley as he stood up from his desk. "How are you both doing?"

Stan and Sue immediately relaxed. The pastor's warm welcoming smile disarmed and encouraged them immediately. "Now tell me, what's on your mind?" he said looking directly at them both.

Stan and Sue looked at each other. "Well, it's the sermon'" said Stan.

"It's our faith," said Sue. Stan looked at Sue."It's what you were saying on Sunday. It all seems to be speaking about us."

"Really? Well let's talk about that," Rev. Manley said encouragingly. He had a constant stream of people through his office since his Sunday sermon. He had asked his secretary to clear his diary for at least the next two weeks, because he expected that many of his people would want to see him.

Stan and Sue explained that they felt their spiritual lives were not what they used to be. Stan said how hard he had found it to pray and read his Bible recently. "Of course," said Rev. Manley, "but no doubt you lead very busy, full lives. It must be hard to do the things that you used to do." Stan and Sue relaxed still more.

There was no hint of condemnation in what their pastor was saying. "But tell me, what about your fears?"

"What do you mean?" said Stan.

"You know, the things that you've worried about, your anxieties, You see, I've found that in the same way that 'perfect love casts out fear' like John says in his first letter, fear comes in when our love for the Lord begins to recede. If your love for him has started to cool off, I would expect that fears have begun to grow."

Stan was silent but Sue said, "Yes, that's right. I am more worried now than I used to be, and funnily enough if I think about it I've got less to worry about."

Rev. Manley looked at her with fatherly eyes. "Well, tell me about it.' She described her fears for the children's safety, her worries about money, and her anxiety about trying to fit everything into her busy life. Stan sat in silence. He did not know any of this and was a little embarrassed that his wife was sharing these things in such an open way.

"That's right," Rev. Manley replied. "That's exactly what's been going on with me. I've busied myself with my own work, and until these last few weeks I've been worried about all kinds of things — things that I can never control or change. But since I came back to the intimate friendship I used to have with the Lord, the worries have begun to recede and have been replaced by the peace I once knew."

"I suppose that's where I am," said Stan. "'Things have slipped and I don't know God's closeness in the way that I used to."

"Well we all need our hearts fixing," observed the pastor. "I've had to ask God to clear out the arteries of my spiritual life and let his Spirit flow again."

"It's funny you should say that," said Stan, "because I make the equipment that does that. It's a catheter through which a tiny balloon is inflated into the artery to open it up and make it work again. Since coming in here I've had this strange pressure building up inside as though God has been doing his very own angioplasty on me."

The Drivers and Rev. Manley met again on several occasions and were able to work through many of their difficulties. But that first meeting provided the breakthrough. Their hearts were mended and their lives were changed.

In the 21st century and especially at the moment during our present crisis we talk about things like stress, anxiety, responsibilities, and more. But actually, the heart of these things is fear. We're just afraid. Fear is a terrible bedfellow because it keeps you awake at night, and makes it impossible for you to focus on the day. As a result, you never really enjoy the blessings of this life because they always have this bitter taste of fear underneath. This is not how Jesus wants us to live! John tells us that perfect love drives out fear. We only find this perfect love in Jesus, and Jesus wants his love that we place first in our life to fill our hearts and drive away the fear.

TO THOSE WHO OVERCOME

Ask God to give you any actions for change you might need to make. In his letter to Ephesus, the Lord promises a particular gift to those who overcome. "To him who overcomes, I will give the right to eat from the tree of life, which is in the paradise of God." The gift is life symbolized by the tree of life that grew in Eden's paradise.

The word paradise means walled garden, usually in a royal palace, and speaks of protection, provision, and play. A walled garden is a place of protection because there is a barrier between us and the outside world. Spiritual protection is one of the fruits of God's life flowing within us. Genesis tells us that God walked in his garden in the cool of the evening. We are at our safest when we walk closely with him.

The tree of life in the paradise of God speaks also of provision. It is God's life and the working of that life within us that feeds and sustains us. We are most likely to grow and to receive spiritual nourishment when we are closest to him.

This image also seems to speak of a playfulness in the heart of God which he wants to pass on to us, his children. The walled garden of the royal palace was called a paradise because it provided a safe place for the inhabitants to enjoy, relax, and be entertained, as well as providing food and protection. It was the place where the children played.

God has a deep desire to see his life bring enjoyment and blessing to his children. His concern for the church in Ephesus and for each of us who find ourselves in danger of losing our first love is not that he does not receive from us what we should give, but that he is unable to give us what we need. The Christians in Ephesus were being called to enter the garden of God's grace and walk with him in the cool of the day, as Adam and Eve once did. They were being called to enjoy life with God in all its abundance.. Jesus calls us to do the same.

CRISIS AND CULTURAL EARTHQUAKES: A TIME TO PAUSE

One of the impacts of the COVID-19 crisis is that many of us were forced to live in quarantine for an extended period. This time of enforced retreat was unusual for most of us. So it brought to mind a lot of questions.

One question that I asked is: What does it mean to embrace our first love for Jesus in a time of crisis or a time of enforced retreat, even when we see it as forced? Jesus is our example, and he shows us what to do. He lived with a pattern of retreat and engagement. Luke 5:16 tells us that "Jesus often withdrew to lonely places and prayed."

What do we learn from his example here? Jesus took time to retreat to engage with God. He was spending time with his first love!

What happened when Jesus did this? He walked with the Holy Spirit and re-engaged with his identity as God's Son. We can do the same ,we can use the time of retreat that we are forced into during crisis to let God's Word and God's Spirit remind us of our identity as children of God. From this identity, we are reminded of the authority God gives us as his covenant emissaries, which leads us to and results in, the power to live as God's children and God's representatives especially when the world is in such chaos and crisis.

Read Luke 4:1-13 to see how Jesus embraced his first love in a time of retreat, and saw it result in authority and power to overcome the temptations of the devil.

HUDDLE STUDY GUIDE
Why is pride so dangerous for a church? Why is it so dangerous for us personally?

How have you seen pride lead you away from your first love for God?

What does Jesus show us about the value of our first love?

2

SMYRNA
A CRISIS OF PERSECUTION

To the angel of the church in Smyrna write:

These are the words of him who is the First and the Last, who died and came to life again. I know your afflictions and your poverty—yet you are rich! I know about the slander of those who say they are Jews and are not, but are a synagogue of Satan. Do not be afraid of what you are about to suffer. I tell you, the devil will put some of you in prison to test you, and you will suffer persecution for ten days. Be faithful, even to the point of death, and I will give you life as your victor's crown.

Whoever has ears, let them hear what the Spirit says to the churches. The one who is victorious will not be hurt at all by the second death.

Revelation 2:8-11

In the spring of 1992 an Episcopal priest named Terry Harri left the Church of the Good Shepherd in Little Rock, Arkansas for a new ministry in Homestead, Florida. On the day he left, it was raining in the jungles of West Africa, as it does every day in the equatorial rain forest. The systems of air currents and moisture that produce these daily rains intensify as the seas around the West African coast warm the air passing overhead.

These occurrences on the other side of the world did not enter Terry's mind as he prepared to leave for his new home. Like most pastors with a new post, he was tremendously excited. I can recall his speaking with enthusiasm about his new home in Florida, the environment, the community and, of course, the climate.

The swirling patterns of winds and clouds flowing from the west coast of Africa pass the Doldrums and enter into the equatorial waters of the Atlantic Ocean. They were thickening and intensifying as Terry began to settle into his new work..For complex reasons beyond our understanding, this disorganised weather system began to gather and unified around a growing low pressure zone. The midsummer sun, heating the waters of the Atlantic, powered the depression as it deepened and extended. A tropical storm began to build. The meteorologists back in America had noticed its development, and the Weather Channel began to track its course. By the time the storm headed for Bermuda, the National Hurricane Center in Miami had upgraded the storm to full hurricane status. Hurricane Andrew had been born.

For a time it seemed as though Andrew would leave Florida untouched as it veered south toward the Caribbean. But this turned out to be a vain hope as the storm reached the coast of America, ripping through the southern tip of Florida and destroying almost everything in its way.

Terry arrived in early spring, and by late summer his new community had been devastated. Homestead, his new home, was completely destroyed.

Fortunately, the architect who designed Terry's church building built it with hurricanes in mind. The building suffered some structural damage but was secure enough to provide shelter for many fleeing from the effects of the storm. However, many buildings nearby were completely destroyed or severely damaged.

The government investigation held in the wake of the disaster revealed that many of the homes and buildings in the Homestead community had been built with poor materials and shoddy workmanship. In a television interview, one of the local residents said that he knew which architects and builders to go to as he thought about rebuilding his home. He would go to the ones who had built houses that had stood in the storm. Already in our post-COVID-19 reality Governments and institutions,businesses and churches are assessing the damage of a world torn by crisis. The weaknesses that were already present in our social fabric have been radically exposed with renewed and radical calls for change especially surrounding racial inequalities.

In the parable of the wise and foolish builders, Jesus tells us that he expects his disciples to follow the example of the wise builder. "Therefore everyone who hears these words of mine and puts them into practice is like a wise man who built his house on the rock" (Matt. 7:24). His house was still standing after the storm. It survived because he built it on the rock. We do the same with our lives when we hear the word of Jesus and put it into practice: "But everyone who hears these words of mine and does not put them into practice is like a foolish man who built his house on sand" (Matt. 7:26). Foolish builders build on sand because they do not act on what they hear.

The church in Smyrna was a church of wise builders. It is an example of a church who learned how to weather the storm-- a church built on the rock. The Christians here were severely afflicted and under the most intense pressure. But because they had built on a secure foundation of Jesus' teaching, they were able to stand.

Within the region Smyrna is one of the few places where a church has continued to exist since New Testament times. Why has this church held on and prospered in the face of persecution? Because it acted on what Jesus had said. These Christians were wise builders.

There are seven letters to seven churches in Revelation, and only two -- Smyrna and Philadelphia-- receive unconditional praise. Most of them receive a mixture of reprimand and encouragement. But the Lord found nothing negative to say about this church. His only word was to hold on and be faithful, and the evidence suggests that they did just that. At the turn of the century, there were still 100,000 people in Smyrna who called themselves Christians. Surely this is the kind of church to which we would want to belong. Even today a modest church still survives, one of very few in modern Turkey.

LIFE IN SMYRNA
The church in Smyrna was set in a large city which lay thirty-five miles due north of Ephesus. It had an ideal position on the Aegean coast. The bay on which it was built provided a superb natural harbor still in use today. Unlike Ephesus, Smyrna is still an important city. Today it is called Izmir and is one of the most important Turkish cities on that coast.

Smyrna was an unusual city in that it was built to a plan. About 300 years before the time of Christ, an extremely wealthy king decided to use an overall strategy in building it. Smyrna became one of the very few cities of antiquity that followed a grid pattern which everyone could understand. Most cities at the time had grown organically with narrow winding streets. Smyrna was the Paris of Asia Minor, built with straight broad avenues and large airy buildings. It protected the natural gulf and harbor on which it was built and provided access to the sea for merchants from the east. Being built on the sloping hillside running down to the sea meant that even in the heights of summer, the winds blowing off the Aegean would keep the city cool and free from the humidity that clogged the air in so many cities at the time. Smyrna was considered to be the most beautiful city of Asia Minor and one of the most beautiful of the ancient world.

Smyrna was known for loyalty as well as beauty. Even before Rome became an imperial power, Smyrna had developed friendly relationships with the Roman senate. By the time Rome became the principal power in the region, Smyrna's unquestioned loyalty had been established. So it was here that the temple to Caesar was built, a kind of imperial stamp of approval. Smyrna was also the site of the annual games where athletes from all round the world gathered to compete. It was for such reasons that by New Testament times, Smyrna had become a rival to Ephesus, vying for the title of first city of Asia Minor.

But the church in Smyrna, unlike that in Ephesus, seems to have been small, weak, and constantly under pressure. The risen Lord said, "'I know your afflictions and your poverty." These Christians were literally penniless. Many had been thrown into prison, and others suffered the severest persecution. We can imagine the pastor of this church taking the final session of their welcome course and saying, "'We're very glad that you're joining us. We'll get you on the church roll and then some of the local thugs will come and take away all your furniture, throw you out of work, beat you up, and you'll live penniless for the rest of your life, however long that might be!" In other words, they were facing a crisis of persecution.

It is clear that the church in the U.S.A. is being stripped. The things that used to form the backbone of common church culture have been removed. Things like live music,that all can participate in,children's work, meeting together in groups larger than 10 have all had to be taken away . Many churches as of summer 2020 are not even considering going back into their buildings until 2021, by then they will have been out of their public gathering space for 9 months. This is a persecution of a completely different kind to anything any of us could have anticipated.

However persecution was the common experience of many during the time this passage was written. Another passage in the New Testament gives a clear picture of what a Christian might expect from life:

Sometimes you were publicly exposed to insult and persecution; at other times you stood side by side with those who were so treated. You sympathized with those in prison and joyfully accepted the confiscation of your property, because you knew that you yourselves had better and lasting possessions (Hebrews 10:33-34).

These Christians in Smyrna also had better and lasting possessions. So Jesus says, "I know your afflictions and your poverty, yet you are rich!" Not rich in the things of the world, but rich in the things that are important. These persecuted Christians were storing up for themselves treasures in heaven where moth and rust cannot destroy and thieves are unable to break in and steal. They were holding lightly to material things, but their grip was firm on the spiritual treasures of everlasting life. They had a biblical value system and they understood what real wealth was all about. They knew that they were precious in God's sight, and this allowed them to hold on to him and freely release everything else.

Persecution had stripped them down to their bare essentials. But instead of slowing their progress, this led them to run the race with perseverance. All the Lord needed to say was "keep going, be faithful and you will receive the winner's crown in the end!" These were encouraging words for people who saw the victory ceremony in the games every year. Like those victors, Smyrnan Christians would receive their crown at the end of the race, and they would receive it from the Lord himself.

As well as perseverance, sufferings produced depth within these Christians. A generation after this letter was written, Polycarp, the bishop of Smyrna, was burned at the stake. But his witness in dying was such that many turned to Christ, and he is still remembered today as one of the great martyrs of the Christian church. This small insignificant group of Christians has touched the world by its faith and obedience. It has weathered the storms and provided a model of how we should build churches today. It was a house built on the rock!

God's plan is that all Christians receive the unequivocal praise he gave to Smyrna and that we continue to grow what- ever the circumstances.

TESTING TIMES

As a young clergyman, I realized that this was what God wanted and so I began a lifetime's work of learning from the churches who had weathered the storms and flourished despite them. The churches of the two-thirds world, so often faced with adversity, are seeing remarkable growth. The storms of life bend and break their communities, and yet there is often incredible growth and spiritual blessing among God's people.

In my reading I have discovered that much of the material that we would call "church growth" is based on the early observations of western missionaries in non western cultures. These observations have produced formulas that many churches and pastors follow, but do they contain the same faith that lies at the heart of what God is doing among these poorer people?

My question has always been why. These churches, like Smyrna, shame us with their faith and perseverance and now are beginning to touch the world with their message. In the years to come we can expect that the leaders of the church in Asia, Africa, and Latin America will have a global impact on the future direction of Christianity. When I have met leaders from these continents, I have often been struck by my own poverty of faith in comparison with the riches that they know. But amid frustration and failure, I have begun to see exciting results, first in inner-city youth work and then in small inner-city congregations. These communities, like those of the third world, are ones where social hurricanes have been blowing for a long time. Yet my discovery is that the church is able to grow and flourish. If the church in other places is to grow like these, it must learn the lessons of these suffering Christians and follow their example. Perhaps COVID-19 is a way in which we can all understand better the challenges of the early church and the persecution it continually faced day in and day out.

EYES TO THE VICTORY

The Christians in Smyrna understood that they needed to
set their sights on God's promises for the future rather than
their circumstances in the present. They were about to suffer
persecution and be tested by the devil, but this time of testing
would not last for long. Ten days is a symbolic language for a
fixed short period of time. The church at Smyrna would be tested
by the devil, but only for a fixed period of time. Jesus is the first
and the last and as such is Lord of all time. He sets the seasons,
and the length that they run, and although the devil may seem to
have his way, the Lord sets parameters to his evil. The church was
told that they were in the middle of a struggle between good and
evil that God would ultimately and certainly win.

When the allied forces invaded continental Europe from their
bases in southern England on June 6, 1944, both the Allied
leaders and the German high command knew that victory had
been secured. A successful D-Day meant that victory, VE Day,
was a certainty. The senior staff on both sides of the conflict
understood this clearly, and yet the Second World War continued
for another eleven months. The plan among a number of Hitler's
generals was to get rid of him, offer strong resistance, and then
sue for peace. The assassination attempt failed, the conspirators
were executed, and the resistance that the German army offered
was as fierce as ever even though they knew their days were
numbered. The retreating German army fought every inch of
the way. In fact more military personnel were lost in the eleven
months between D-Day and VE Day than at any other time in
the war. Added to this, the SS, masters of the Nazi death camps,
attempted to kill even more Jews during this period. The Allied
victory was secure and yet the struggle against a foe furious in
defeat was as intense as ever.

D-Day for the Christian church began with the incarnation of the Son of God. The bridgehead was secured with his death and resurrection. Since that time, the Kingdom of God has been moving forward in the power of the Holy Spirit, struggling against the kingdom of darkness, waiting for our victory day when Christ returns. Our struggles against these evil powers are as intense as any of those in the Second World War. We are not fighting against flesh and blood but against the spiritual rulers of this dark world. This struggle involves suffering and hardship for all those called to participate in the fight. At times it will involve persecution and death, but Christ assures us that we will not be touched by the "second death" — eternal separation from God — if we hold on and trust him to the end.

The remarkable thing, and one of the great mysteries of the universe, is that God is able to use these times of testing to strengthen our faith, deepen our character, and increase our usefulness to him in his Kingdom. The result of testing is a faithful, strong church, unafraid of the devil, able to rejoice and witness in all circumstances. One of the ways in which testing produces growth in a Christian's life is that we learn to have a heavenward perspective. Our life then focuses on working toward the victory that Christ will bring at his Second Coming. Short-term difficulties and defeats will not deflect us if we have a determination that grows from the promise of Christ's return.

In China, Christianity, like all other religions, was severely persecuted during the Cultural Revolution, and although the others were almost completely exterminated, the church grew. When the communists came and the missionaries left, the Chinese church numbered little more than half a million. Today, fifty years later, there are more Christians in China than there are people living in the British isles. Millions and millions have come to know the Lord through a persecuted church — a church which suffered the imprisonment and death of its leaders, the closure of its buildings and the loss of its property — a church which held on against the odds and saw victory in the midst of apparent defeat.

CIRCUMSTANTIAL PERSECUTION

The COVID-19 crisis is not a persecution perpetrated by a group or an institution against the church but in many ways the effects on the gathered Church is the same. In his remarkable book Anti fragile by Naseem Talebhe has given us a new vocabulary by which to understand this remarkable phenomenon so present in Smyrna and in many persecuted churches throughout history.

Anti fragile is the opposite of fragile. It is a structure or system that actually thrives and grows under pressure.

Fragile structures and systems collapse under stress

Robust structures and systems resist for a while then collapse.

Anti fragile structures and systems thrive and prosper in difficult and extreme conditions.

The church in Smyrna was anti -fragile.

I wonder how we will manifest anti fragility as we emerge into our post-COVID-19 reality. What will have thrived and grown under these stressful and unexpected circumstances.

The devil is the author of our testing. God allows it because he is able to use it for our growth and the benefit of the world. He is able to turn the most evil of intentions and use them for his greater purposes to bless us and save the world. He has shown this most perfectly by turning the apparent failure and foolishness of the cross to the victory and celebration of the resurrection.

PREPARED TO WITHSTAND

A story I heard illustrates this well. A man traveling in the wilderness of Canada found himself watching lumberjacks as they worked. One particularly took his interest. His spiked boots were helping him walk from tree to tree as they floated down the river. His job was to clear the log jams using a long pole with a hook on the end. As he freed the jam, he appeared to select one or two trees for some special purpose. Every so often he hooked a log and pushed it to the side out of the flow of the current. During the lumberjack's lunch break, the observer asked, "What are you doing?"

"I'm looking for the particular trees that I want to use to build my house," the lumberjack replied.

"What are you looking for?"

"I'm looking for the trees that grow at the top of the mountains. Up there, there are storms all year round and huge differences in temperature." He went on to explain that the rings on these trees were very tightly packed and the quality of the wood very high. The trees that had grown in the most difficult circumstances were now the strongest. These were the trees he wanted to build his house.

Haggai the prophet, who called the people of Israel to rebuild the Temple, understood this because he said, "'Go up into the mountains and bring down timber and build the house, so that I may take pleasure in it and be honored,'" says the Lord" (Hag. 1:8). We grow strongest in the face of the sternest opposition, as the biographies of great men and women often testify. We grow strongest when times are hard, but we forget this when times are easy. In the midst of testing and difficulty, we need to remind ourselves of these truths.

I can look back with thankfulness for the ways in which difficult experiences and hard testing have produced good things in my life. I am not grateful for the awful things themselves, but for the way in which God was able to use them for his purposes and my benefit. My wife and I are even at the stage where we can laugh about difficult times past and rejoice in the lessons we have learned. The most important times of growth have often been times of greatest pain. Of course, I rarely knew it at the time, but now I can look back and marvel at how God used them.

One year particularly springs to mind. It included the birth of our first child, who was thought to have a hole in the heart. My wife was examined for breast cancer, two cars were written off, a beloved grandmother died, and I was taken into hospital for plastic surgery after receiving third-degree burns on my legs. Even our dog had to be put down! Calamity seemed to mark our everyday experience, and yet undoubtedly this was the spiritual watershed of our lives. It provided us with the spiritual breakthrough which has produced untold blessings since.

As well as my own testimony I have witnessed this in the lives of many others. Working in the inner city brings you into contact with some amazing people — apparently damaged and broken by the continual pressure of circumstance and anxiety but who, in God's hands, have been used to extraordinary effect. As a vicar in Brixton, I was fortunate to meet people whom the world had rejected. These same people had developed such deep confidence and rich character that in the church God could use them as examples of what he could do. Some of them could hardly read or write and yet were used to deliver God's word in powerful ways.

Others were thought of as oddities and yet were able to touch the lives of many people through their simple trust in God.

So it is in the kingdom! God is far less interested in worldly status than in humble service — less interested in human talent than in faithful witness. Those who have held onto God when there is nothing else to hold on to are able to teach us what holding on is all about. Like Susan who held on to God's love despite an alcoholic husband who returned to their home to beat her and terrorized the children — or like Jason who found the courage to share his faith with his drug- addicted parents who had abandoned him on the streets as a child. These Christians, like so many others, have discovered that when there is no one to turn to, God is always there.

Dependence on him gives rise to faithfulness. Often we need to be taken to the brink of disaster to be taught what dependence on him is all about. We all recognize those who keep their head and hold their faith when all others are losing theirs. These have experienced God's help in need and his rescue in disaster. They have developed strong faith and have found God to be utterly trustworthy on every occasion.

While I was the Pastor of St Thomas church Sheffield we grew and developed a city expression of the church in a downtown night club. It was fantastic and we saw the congregation transform this ugly , dirty building into a wonderful place of worship.

People loved the place and more and more people came and joined us there.

One day the fire marshal walked around the building and out of the blue closed us down due to several fire and safety violations which we had no idea about and could not afford to rectify

It was a shock and we were never able to go back into the building to worship again.

However because of the other structures we had in place within the church which we called house churches , we were able to meet without a central gathering space for 18 months and still grow and our giving even grew too.

We were really surprised and very thankful. This very specific and sudden persecution which meant we had to go "underground" did not cause us to shrink back but rather embrace it and thrive .

THE JOY OF TESTING

James, in his letter, says, "Consider it pure joy, my brothers, whenever you face trials of many kinds, because you know that the testing of your faith develops perseverance. Perseverance must finish its work so that you may be mature and complete, not lacking anything" (James 1:2-4). When we are tested, we discover what we are made of. We find out how much the Lord has put in us. It is as though the foundations of our life can have both rock and sand. By testing and difficulty, the Lord removes the insubstantial sand in our foundations and reveals the rock of Jesus and his word. At first we find this process difficult, but with time and a right understanding of what is happening, we can more actively enter into the process and even get to the stage where we consider it pure joy. The more we are able to see testing in this positive light, the more mature we are, which probably means that we have seen a lot of testing already!

Jesus tells the Christians in Smyrna, "'Be faithful, even to the point of death, and I will give you the crown of life." He wants us to continue in the midst of suffering hardship and difficulty, and as we run the race he holds out the victor's crown. The word crown is the wreath — in Greek the *stephanos* — that is presented to the winner at the end of a race. The people of Smyrna understood athletics. They knew that only those who continued steadfastly to the end could be expected to be.acclaimed as victorious. The Lord encourages them and us to do this.

It is said that a man stranded on a desert island scanned the horizon daily for evidence of a ship that might come to save him. In time he built a makeshift home from the materials he had salvaged from the wreck — but still he watched and waited. One day, while away from his camp, he noticed a wisp of smoke and ran to investigate. He found his home and all his possessions on fire. In the depth of depression he gave up, assuming that the end was near. The next morning a rowing boat approached the beach to rescue him. When they reached him, the men said, "We saw your signal fire yesterday, but the tide was against us and so we could not come until this morning."

God will never forsake us. He will always come with his rescue. In whatever circumstances we face, "'Let us hold unswervingly to the hope we profess, for he who promised is faithful" (Hebrews 10:23).

CRISIS AND CULTURAL EARTHQUAKES: SHAKABLE OR UNSHAKABLE

The crisis of persecution can create a seismic event in our lives and in our church communities. Likewise, the COVID-19 pandemic created a seismic event in our lives. So how do we respond to this kind of crisis? We can look to the Bible for examples from Christians in the past. For example, the people who received the letter of Hebrews were probably living in the wake of General Titus' destruction of Jerusalem, which scattered the Jews (also called Hebrews) all over the known world. So the writer to the Hebrews addressed this kind of shaking in Hebrews 12.

You have not come to a mountain that can be touched and that is burning with fire; to darkness, gloom and storm; to a trumpet blast or to such a voice speaking words that those who heard it begged that no further word be spoken to them, because they could not bear what was commanded: "If even an animal touches the mountain, it must be stoned to death." The sight was so terrifying that Moses said, "I am trembling with fear."

But you have come to Mount Zion, to the city of the living God, the heavenly Jerusalem. You have come to thousands upon thousands of angels in joyful assembly, to the church of the firstborn, whose names are written in heaven. You have come to God, the Judge of all, to the spirits of the righteous made perfect, to Jesus the mediator of a new covenant, and to the sprinkled blood that speaks a better word than the blood of Abel.

See to it that you do not refuse him who speaks. If they did not escape when they refused him who warned them on earth, how much less will we, if we turn away from him who warns us from heaven? At that time his voice shook the earth, but now he has promised, "Once more I will shake not only the earth but also the heavens." The words "once more" indicate the removing of what can be shaken—that is, created things—so that what cannot be shaken may remain.

> *Therefore, since we are receiving a kingdom that cannot be shaken, let us be thankful, and so worship God acceptably with reverence and awe, for our "God is a consuming fire."*

Hebrews 12:18-29

As we face the circumstances of a crisis like persecution or like what we all experienced during the pandemic, we need to ask ourselves what is being shaken and what is revealed as unshakable and anti fragile. Created things are shakeable--our jobs, our routines, and even our emotions and our physical health. But if our faith is in things that are unshakable, we will experience peace even in crisis. We will return to our identity as God's children and representatives. And we will learn what God wants to reveal about unshakable things in his Kingdom.

HUDDLE STUDY GUIDE

How do you respond when you are tested? What makes you see the test as persecution or as judgment or as pruning?

Anti fragile means our communities should thrive during crisis, how does your family, church and community do under stress.

What does victory look like in the midst of persecution? Does it mean escaping persecution or something else? What examples of victory have you seen or experienced?

How can we focus on God's faithfulness in the midst of persecution or other crises? How can we do this in community?

3

PERGAMUM
A CRISIS OF COMPROMISE

To the angel of the church in Pergamum write:

These are the words of him who has the sharp, double-edged sword. I know where you live—where Satan has his throne. Yet you remain true to my name. You did not renounce your faith in me, not even in the days of Antipas, my faithful witness, who was put to death in your city—where Satan lives.

Nevertheless, I have a few things against you: There are some among you who hold to the teaching of Balaam, who taught Balak to entice the Israelites to sin so that they ate food sacrificed to idols and committed sexual immorality. Likewise, you also have those who hold to the teaching of the Nicolaitans. Repent therefore! Otherwise, I will soon come to you and will fight against them with the sword of my mouth.

Whoever has ears, let them hear what the Spirit says to the churches. To the one who is victorious, I will give some of the hidden manna. I will also give that person a white stone with a new name written on it, known only to the one who receives it.

Revelation 2:12-17

Compromise is a factor in all our lives. We are called to compromise almost every day. At times this is necessary and good. Finding solutions to knotty problems often requires people who are prepared to compromise. Negotiation between two parties occurs at every level of our social life--everything from working out a pay deal to what time the kids go to bed.

However there are times when compromise is very unhelpful e.g. we may find ourselves in situations at work or among our neighbors where classist,racist or sexist views and opinions are regularly expressed. What should we do? We want to maintain the relationship with these people otherwise our influence and witness may be removed forever.

My main approach is to show through my body language and my face that I want to be open to these friends but to say nothing that would ever support the views expressed and then if I am asked to comment I simply say very humbly and respectfully that my view is one of equality and fairness and justice. This is difficult but with practise it really can work both to stand your ground and keep the relationships.

Compromise was the problem at Pergamum. This was the challenge that the church faced daily and one which the Lord wanted to teach them about.

LIFE IN PERGAMUM

Pergamum was the Roman capital of the region, but it had few natural assets that enabled it to function as a capital city. It was a long distance from the sea, commanding few principal trade routes, and yet over the centuries it had developed first under the Attalid empire, and then as the Roman empire, as the administrative center for the region.

In addition to government, Pergamum had two other specialties. The first was education. Pergamum was inextricably tied to its libraries and parchments. It had one of the great libraries of the world, containing more than two hundred thousand scrolls. Even its name was a development of the common word used for parchment. It was a city of learning and books.

The other speciality was religion. Pergamum had more temples per capita than anywhere else in the region. There were temples and religious sites dedicated to almost every god in the Greco-Roman pantheon. The great temple of Athena crowned the Acropolis that stood behind the city, and a huge altar to Zeus was also found there. But the principal religion of the city was Caesar worship. The cult of the emperors was strongest in this seat of imperial power. No less than three temples were dedicated to Caesar, and it was expected in this center of Roman influence and power that loyalty to Rome would be expressed as worship, offered in these temples daily.

THE PLACE OF PERSECUTION

In Pergamum the imperial power of Rome was unchallenged. The Romans insisted on complete obedience and loyalty to the empire. This could be expressed in a number of ways, but none more important than burning incense to Caesar. Worshipping in this way indicated a person's submission to Rome and citizenship of the empire. A Christian's refusal would be seen not as conscientious avoidance but as outright rebellion. Still, most Christians in Pergamum chose to make a stand and not burn incense to the image of Caesar.

Confronted by this kind of resistance, the Romans answered with persecution. By persecuting the Christians, they hoped to contain the rebellion to a small group and create sufficient fear to stop the spread of what to them was dangerous insubordination. To this end, Roman authorities spread all kinds of myths. They took the common teaching of the church and twisted it so that in the minds of ordinary people the Christians only got what they deserved.

For instance, it was rumored that the church was incestuous because there was love between brothers and sisters. They were called cannibals because they regularly ate the body and blood of their leader, and they were unpatriotic because they would not worship the emperor as a god. The Roman authorities had no problem with Christians worshipping their own God, as long as they also recognized the divinity of Caesar and included him in their regular schedule of worship.

Christians in Pergamum were under the intense pressure. They felt the full effects of the unbridled power of Rome. Persecution was not simply a possibility, but a daily reality which placed the average believer under enormous strain. Already Antipas, one of their number, had been roasted alive in the presence of his persecutors and supporters. Tradition tells us that a fire was set under one of the bronze bulls that stood outside one of the temples in Pergamum. The bull was opened, and Antipas was forced inside and left to die a slow death that delighted the authorities and horrified the church. The life expectancy of a Christian living in Pergamum could not have been very long. The demonically inspired power that persecuted had fine-tuned their torture to produce the greatest pain and instil the deepest fear.

But as so often with these devilish plots, the Romans offered a way out. All believers needed was to do their duty as good citizens and burn incense to Caesar in his temple. What harm could come from that? If they did this small act of obedience, they would be left in peace by those in power, and would be free to conduct their lives as they saw fit. This small compromise would ensure a life free from the pressure of persecution.

The church was divided. Some said they could not conscientiously witness the sovereignty of God and still worship Caesar. Others found an alternative that seemed to allow Christians to comply with the government's request, while at the same time preserving their integrity. This second group called themselves the Nicolaitans, and they offered a solution to the crisis the church faced.

THE COMPROMISE OF THE NICOLAITANS
Using the popular philosophy of the day, they taught that people were divided into body and spirit, into an inner and outer life. Only the spirit was valuable to God. Only the spirit affected the spiritual realm, and that realm was completely detached from the corrupt physical realm in which the body lived: Therefore Christians could burn incense to Caesar with their bodies and keep their spirits pure and wholly surrendered to God.

Nicolaitians thought that surely nothing was wrong in seeking peace and protection for themselves and their families if this could be achieved by doing something that did not compromise their spiritual life. As long as the heart was given to Jesus, as long as the will was„surrendered to him, as long as the spirit was given to God, did it matter if their bodies appeared to be offering worship to Caesar? After all, real worship begins in the heart. True prayer flows from the soul of a person and reaches God who himself is a spirit. Outward bodily functions therefore were believed to be unimportant and could be ignored.

This deception deepened as biblical sounding phrases were added to the argument. "'We know that Jesus is King. We know that there is only one God and that the idol, whether it be of Zeus or of the emperor, is nothing but an image. Everybody knows the idol is not real and not a god, so sing a song to Jesus, pray to the Lord, and do your patriotic duty!'"

To people suffering the kinds of pressure that the Christians in Pergamum were under, this teaching sounded very attractive and came as a great relief. It seemed that the way they could avoid persecution legitimately was to use this understanding of material and spiritual reality. It appears that many adopted what the Nicolaitans were saying.

The devil had cleverly conceived a plan that would compromise and corrupt the church. By the use of intense persecution on the one hand and subtle deception on the other, he brought many Christians to the conclusion that this new teaching was the rational way to conduct their life within the context of the Roman empire. He made it look as though the church could be left to continue its witness and work for the extension of God's kingdom without unnecessary fear of persecution and death.

STANDING UNDER PRESSURE
The problem with pressure is that we tend to embrace the first escape that is offered. One of Satan's strategies is to apply pressure and then release it in the hope that Christians will surrender to

their own inclinations and follow the route he is providing. But the Lord calls us to steadfastness under pressure and to a level of personal commitment and holiness that will prevent us from taking the line of least resistance.

The Christians in Pergamum were under pressure from all sides. The teaching of the Nicolaitans lifted the pressure from one direction, and those who followed this attractive, and apparently reasonable, teaching fell into compromise and sin, simply because they were looking for a way out rather than a way to stand.

To illustrate this I once invited a young man to come forward in church. Then I and another man pushed from front and back, and we asked him to resist with all his strength, tensing all his muscles to hold out against the pressure I was exerting on his chest and the other man was exerting on his back. He was resisting well until I removed my hands, and without any more pressure he simply fell over. Organized, officially sanctioned, persecution is not common in the western world, and yet some churches do suffer a similar pressure from their local governments and city councils. Many churches have sought official funding and grant aid for community projects and have been offered the money as long as they compromise their core values.

Faced with the option of funding or financial need, some churches compromise their position. Others hold out and at times pay the penalty of seeing projects and programs fall. The call to compromise and the pressure of persecution may be more subtle, but nevertheless just as real.

When we lived in Arkansas, I discovered that clergymen pay their tax once a year. This is fine as long as you have saved it up. I am not particularly good with numbers, so my wife, Sally, has generally taken care of that side of our household management.

We had to pay $200 more than we expected because the government changed the way they taxed clergymen. Then, just as we were leaving the States to return to England, we heard that we had to pay another $1300 on top of that. My immediate reaction was not to pay. I was leaving the country after all. Of course, I quickly thought better and paid up, but the temptation was certainly there.

We are constantly given the opportunity to be dishonest, if not with our taxes then with our employer's property, if not with our actions, then with the truth. Compromise is always an option, but the consequences of compromise can be dire.

There's a story of the goose that flew south with the flock every winter. One year it noticed down in the farmyard that some other geese were not flying with them. As he looked down, he thought, "They look happy and healthy." So he flew down and began feeding on the grain the other geese were eating. He stayed there the whole winter. When he saw that the flock was flying north again, he struggled to catch up to them. Somehow he had put on weight during the winter. He quickly realized how difficult it was going to be to fly with the flock, and so he said, 'I'll catch you up next time you pass,' and he flew back to the farmyard. He never noticed next time they passed. In fact he was too busy eating. He never saw them again — he was being fattened up for the oven.

Compromise is a deadly option. It may seem the most reasonable alternative at the time, but in the end it can only lead to spiritual decline and death. As with the Christians in Pergamum, fighting compromise is a daily struggle. For the people in Pergamum, the call to compromise came from many quarters and presented itself in many disguises.

There are two kinds of compromise. The first is a compromise with power; this is the kind of compromise we have already looked at. The second is a compromise with the permissive society.

COMPROMISE WITH PAGANISM

In Pergamum paganism was rife and daily assaulted the church with the temptation to moral laxity. In Revelation 2 Lord Jesus confronts this temptation when he describes it using the code names of Balaam and Balak.

Balak was the king of Moab during the time that God led Moses and the children of Israel through the wilderness. Balaam was a fortune teller and soothsayer from the land around the Tigris and Euphrates rivers. His reputation had become so great that Balak invited him to Moab to fulfil a special commission. Balak was afraid of the strength of Israel and had seen what they had done to the Amalekites in battle, and so he wanted Balaam to curse the children of Israel and prevent them from prospering any further and pressurizing him and his people.

God told Balaam not to go, but finally, after many requests, allowed Balaam to fulfil his desire to respond to the call of Balak. Even though he was allowed to go, God left no doubt as to how he viewed his persistence in this matter. On his journey to Moab, Balaam's donkey was given the ability to speak to challenge Balaam's headlong pursuit of this folly. (This story should be a great comfort to preachers. If God can use a donkey to preach, he should be able to use us too!)

When Balaam finally arrived, he went with Balak to a high place to see the children of Israel spread out on the plain below. He was unable to curse them because God prevented him, and although he attempted a number of times to fulfil this request, he was unable to do it and so returned to his own land in failure. At that point the Bible becomes silent about the story of Balaam and Balak. Jewish tradition says that Balaam sent word to Balak suggesting that he send the women of Moab to lead the men of Israel into sexual sin. This in turn would lead them to worship the gods of Moab and so bring the wrath of God upon them. The same tradition suggests that this is what lies behind the story found in Numbers 25 where God punishes his people because of their sinful desires and their surrender to the temptation to run after both the women and the gods of the Moabites.

The people in Pergamum had similar temptations. Pagan worship often involved explicitly sexual practices and encouraged immoral behavior such as the use of male and female temple prostitutes. Paganism has always tended toward immoral practices and has often challenged the people of God in their call to a pure life. I always smile at the social anthropologists, historians, and archaeologists who say "Wasn't this a glorious culture!" as they uncover wall paintings and beautiful artefacts from ancient pagan cultures. These societies may have produced good artists, but these people also sacrificed their children to their gods and did unspeakable things to one another.

The prevalent philosophy of the day which provided the Nicolaitan heresy with its system of thought, also allowed for Christian belief and pagan practice to go hand in hand. The dislocation between body and spirit -- an idea that came from Greek philosophers like Aristotle and Plato, not from God -- meant that a person's spiritual life was not affected by behavior or practice. Bodies only provided a container for the pure spiritual reality within, and so morality was an unnecessary burden that could not improve or touch the life of the spirit, and so could be discarded.

By accepting this teaching, first century Christians did not need to feel the sting of marginalization. If their friends were going to have a good time out at the temple on Saturday night, they could go too and still go to church on Sunday with a clear conscience. These people were seduced by simple invitations. They were invited to a party at the local hotspot such as the temple of Zeus. Dancing, alcohol, and drugs were available, and men and women who were clearly unattached. The idea was that as you danced and drank you had a better and better time until eventually all the cares of the world lifted from your shoulders. But the usual conclusion was an out-and-out orgy.

This was a regular event in every city, every community down at the temple, having fun every weekend. The Christians were invited as well, and it seems that some accepted the invitation. This degree of compromise seems shocking to us as believers today, and yet the same call and pressures are upon us constantly.

EVER-PRESENT PAGANISM

Paganism has never gone away. It is one of the underpinning strategies of Satan. It has always been there and it always will until the Lord returns. For instance, teenagers and young adults often find themselves unwittingly involved in behavior that borders on pagan practice. The clarion call of our society is to liberate yourself and experience everything you can as long as you hurt no one.

As Christians, like everyone else within our culture, we are invited to have our desires met by what the culture can provide. We are tempted to satiate our appetites, ambition, and need for approval over almost anything else. When we seem reluctant to join in to the things others do to meet these desires, we can often be challenged for our outdated — even Victorian — views.

This unremitting pressure has a corrosive effect in the lives of immature and vulnerable Christians. As a church leader I deal with scores of young people struggling with issues that are created by the challenge of our contemporary society. We should allow ourselves to be neither overrun nor afraid. When we are overrun, we find it difficult to say no. When we are afraid, we tend to hide from reality. What we must do is continue to stand and without judgmentalism offer the solid alternative of living a life full of the love, peace and joy of the Lord Jesus.

The pressure for moral compromise is just as real today as it was in the time of the New Testament church. We are constantly bombarded by visual and audio media that package and sell an alternative to Christian lifestyle. Much of this is directed at the young and affects those who are most vulnerable and susceptible to influence.

A common problem for Christians trying to communicate the gospel with those who are not Christians is choosing methods that will relate to ordinary people. We may rightly seek to use a non-judgmental approach and create an environment where non-Christians will feel most at home, but this needs to be done with caution if we are not to compromise our beliefs.

A good friend of mine, Hugh Halter, says that Christians need to learn how to throw a good party but one where we serve and don't consume.

Sally and I lived for a few years in Greenville and we used to throw a happy hour Friday night party every week with fun times and great conversations around a firepit outside on our front lawn. This became a much looked forward to gathering place in our neighborhood which we then transferred to' Made it through Monday' weekly family meals, we were called to serve this community and it was very effective because we didn't compromise our beliefs in doing so.

Even though Christians are children of light, compromise will allow us to collude with the most foreign and unchristian spiritual values. When you go into a movie theater, it is at first difficult to see in the dim lighting, but after a time our eyes adapt so that by the time we come out into the daylight, our eyes hurt because of the brightness all around. That's what it's like when we collude with spiritual darkness. It is only when we come into the full light-of Christ again that we realize how dark it was.

The pressures to conform or compromise are as real today as they ever were. Satan's methods may be more subtle and less aggressive, and the cost of persecution may not be as high, but nevertheless, his invitation remains the same. The Christians in Pergamum were called to repent -- to change their mind and turn around. The same challenge lays before us today.

Repentance requires that we first stop what we are doing, but to stop we must recognize the warning signs. A friend of mine named Don Crossland, who heads the Christian ministry Journey to Wholeness, told me once that he uses the simple acronym HALT. This stands for Hungry, Angry, Lonely, or Tired. He says these are the usual warning signs that tell us to slow down and consider our actions carefully.

We have all been designed and built with appetites for nourishment, nurture, and intimacy. These may be emotional or physical needs that can lead us to seek satisfaction without discerning whether the method of satisfaction is the most helpful. For instance, we may have physical hunger pangs, but this does not mean that we should eat high fat, unhealthy food, just because we are hungry. We may recognize a need for physical intimacy, but this does not mean that we should satisfy that need at any cost.

SATISFACTION

Our appetites are triggers that often set in motion behavior that in the end we find is destructive. The answer is to recognize the appetite, identify the need, and stop to consider the options available to us. A verse that has helped me is Psalm 103:5 where we see that God will "satisfy your desires with good things." The Bible is full of this truth. Many of the Psalms speak of our appetites -- physical, emotional, spiritual -- being met by God and him alone.

As she celebrated her miraculous pregnancy, Mary, the mother of Jesus, said, "He has filled the hungry with good things." God is always presented as our provider in the Bible. He alone can meet our needs — and protect us from the consequences of our own desires.

When Jesus called the church in Pergamum to repent, he was asking them to stop, turn around, and change the way they thought. This means that we need to ask God to change our mind. How will he do that? He will come with his Spirit to renew us. He will come with his Spirit of holiness to set our mind apart for him.

Compromise involves surrender to pressure. Interestingly, just as compromise involves surrender, so steadfastness in the face of pressure also involves surrender -- the surrender to Jesus. When we feel the pressure to compromise, instead of giving up, we surrender to Jesus and ask him to meet our needs and strengthen us to stand in the midst of crisis. It may involve a struggle, but fighting compromise is much better than fighting God.

SIN AND THE SWORD

Jesus said that he would come to the church in Pergamum with
a sword and fight those who were leading the church astray:
"Repent therefore! Otherwise, I will soon come to you and will
fight against them with the sword of my mouth." Of course, the
sword symbolizes his Word, but by using such a symbol he wants
us to recognize that he is deadly serious and the issue involves life
and death.

Think back to Shadrach, Meschach, and Abednego being thrown
into the fiery furnace. While they are in the midst of the flames,
Jesus comes with his sword. This sword has two purposes--
judgment and salvation. This reminds us that God is not simply
out to get us. He is saving us with his sword.

At first Jesus will come with his sword and gently prod the areas
of compromise and the unrecognized sinful behavior patterns that
they stem from. John Wesley called them our darling sins-- pet
sins that we harbor, hoping that nobody will notice. These prods
in our conscience are often Jesus saying "I want to put that sin to
death." Often we respond as if we are being asked to surrender
our pet cat to be slaughtered, protecting it and shrinking back.
In the end, however, Jesus will have his way and although we lose
our pet, we are free to have our needs met by God.

A friend of mine told me of a time in Sarawak when he was
serving with the armed forces. They were driving along a jungle
track in three-ton trucks. The convoy had become somewhat
spread out and the lead truck, some way ahead of the others, ran
over a large object in the road. The driver got out to see if there
was any damage and to check what had been squashed beneath

the wheels. He found a huge snake that was over twenty feet long. As he crouched to look at what he thought was a dead animal, it suddenly coiled itself around him and began to squeeze him. When the next truck arrived, the driver was close to death, and only the quick work and sharp knife of the following driver saved his life.

When God comes to put a particular sin of ours to death, he will show us the ugliness and self-indulgence of this sinful behavior and make it so repellent that we will never want to go near it again. The pet is seen for the monstrous parasite that it really is. Instead of the sweet kitten, soft to the touch, soothing us by its presence, we see a giant python squeezing our life from us. Jesus is deadly serious about sin and so should we be. Sin took Jesus to the cross, and because he defeated it there and left it in the grave, it is incompatible with the resurrection life that he gives us. As he continues to bring life to us and death to our sin, he delivers us from its effects and leads us more and more into the life that he has given.

We began this chapter with compromise and ended with sin. That is always the process. If we do not accept the challenge to deal with compromise, we will have to surrender to the process that deals with our sin. Fortunately for us, God is loving and kind and will offer rescue, forgiveness and a fresh start each time we surrender to him, reject compromise and run from sin.

CRISIS AND CULTURAL EARTHQUAKES: COURAGE OVER COMPROMISE

What are we supposed to do when everything shakes? Do we compromise what we believe to try to protect ourselves? We see in the message to Pergamum that this is not the way Jesus wants us to act. We must lead out of faith not fear, never has this been

more applicable than during 2020 when so many have been filled
with fear. Fear of man, fear of dying, fear of not making the right
decisions.

To lead out of faith requires courage and courage comes by
hearing God's voice and acting on it. This is the safe rock to stand
on when all those around you are drowning.

Some will find themselves under severe pressure to compromise
and collude with other peoples fears. Fears that go beyond healthy
caution and wise behaviour, fears about the world being out of
control and God being unable to be Sovereign.

Some may be tempted to collude with frustration instead,
frustration that goes beyond the normal and instead sits at odds
with your neighbor and then leads us to act unlovingly towards
them.

We are called to live by faith and to lead from a secure position of
faith.

The reality of our hearts is that during times of crisis, our natural
instincts for survival lead us to default to self-orientation. Often,
this focus on ourselves leads to fear, and out of this fear we are
tempted to compromise. But when we use crisis as a forced
retreat, and take time to focus on our true identity as God's
children and our authority as God's representatives, then we can
react in a better way. We don't see ourselves as victims of the crisis
but as the people whom God is raising up to be the solution
to the crisis. We are the rescue team in the midst of the world's
suffering, working with God to let his Kingdom come on earth as
it is in heaven.

This clarity about our identity gives us confidence that God is with us. With that confidence, we can respond with courage instead of with compromise. And so we can be bold and courageous Kingdom rescue team members, instead of fearful compromisers.

> *God has said,*
> > *"Never will I leave you;*
> > *never will I forsake you.*
>
> *So we say with confidence,*
> > *"The Lord is my helper; I will not be afraid*
> > *What can mere mortals do to me?"*

Hebrews 13:5-6

HUDDLE STUDY GUIDE

When are you most tempted to compromise? What are you feeling when this happens?

How can you look to God to satisfy you instead of compromising? What are some practical things you can do? How can you do this in community?

How does God view sin? Why is it important for us to understand God's approach to sin? How does this reality change the way we view compromise? How does it change the way we view our appetites?

Do you have people in your life to whom you are accountable?

FOR ADDITIONAL REFLECTION

Who is at the center of your universe? So much in our world tries to make you believe that your needs, wants, desires, and aspirations are at the very heart of your identity. But when we think this way, we take up residence in the center of our universe, instead of putting God there. The next thing that happens is that we all have different truths, because I'm at the center of my universe and you're at the center of yours. Now truth is relative because it's defined by who's at the center of your universe.

How have you seen this happen? How have you experienced this in your life? Reflect on this and then discuss it with your Huddle, to discover what God is saying to you and what you need to do about it.

4

THYATIRA
A CRISIS OF DECEPTION

To the angel of the church in Thyatira write:

These are the words of the Son of God, whose eyes are like blazing fire and whose feet are like burnished bronze. I know your deeds, your love and faith, your service and perseverance, and that you are now doing more than you did at first.

Nevertheless, I have this against you: You tolerate that woman Jezebel, who calls herself a prophet. By her teaching she misleads my servants into sexual immorality and the eating of food sacrificed to idols. I have given her time to repent of her immorality, but she is unwilling. So I will cast her on a bed of suffering, and I will make those who commit adultery with her suffer intensely, unless they repent of her ways. I will strike her children dead. Then all the churches will know that I am he who searches hearts and minds, and I will repay each of you according to your deeds.

Now I say to the rest of you in Thyatira, to you who do not hold to her teaching and have not learned Satan's so-

called deep secrets, 'I will not impose any other burden on
you, except to hold on to what you have until I come.'

To the one who is victorious and does my will to the end,
I will give authority over the nations— that one 'will
rule them with an iron scepter and will dash them to
pieces like pottery'—just as I have received authority from
my Father. I will also give that one the morning star.
Whoever has ears, let them hear what the Spirit says to
the churches.

Revelation 2:18-29

I woke around eight. The children were already up and dressed, and Sally said that she would take the kids down to breakfast and I could sleep in if I wanted to. We were staying in a hotel on the Greek island of Zakinthos. We were having a lovely time swimming and sitting in the sun and eating wonderful Greek food, but today I was surprisingly sleepy and decided that I would take the opportunity that Sally had offered. I went back to sleep and had a remarkably vivid dream.

I was standing in an open courtyard surrounded by the streets of Crookes in Sheffield. Behind me extended the semi-circular canopy of a Victorian railway station, something like York station. From the streets and houses people began to gather into the courtyard. They were sad and sullen- faced. I asked one — a young woman — what was going on.

She said that the Nine O'Clock Service had just closed down and everybody was grieving because of it. She and the others seemed to be making their way toward the railway station, and as she moved on I asked her what she would do now She said that they would all leave for a couple of years, some to travel, some to go home, some to take up different jobs and others to further their education, but that I would see them return again once they were healed.

I woke as Sally returned from breakfast. Instead of being sleepy and leaden-limbed, I was very much awake and ready to get on with the day. As I dressed I told Sally about my dream. She asked whether I thought it was significant. I said I did not know other than that it was amazingly clear,that God was trying to tell me something. For the remaining few days of the holiday I returned to the dream and reflected on what it might mean. I had a growing apprehension within myself that something was happening to which I needed to attend.

On my return from Greece this apprehension was very strong, and so when I arrived at the Manchester Airport, I took the first opportunity to call the church and see what was happening. I spoke to Paddy Mallon, one of the other ministers on the staff, and the first thing he told me was that the Nine O'Clock Service had been closed down by the Bishop of Sheffield and that this had been announced to the Nine O'Clock Service on Thursday, the day of my dream. I hurried home and was able to meet with the other leaders of the church that night to decide a plan.

The Nine O'Clock Service (NOS) had been part of St Thomas' until January 1992. I arrived as the new minister of St Thomas' in June 1994, by which time our connection with NOS had become quite remote. Like many people I knew of the reputation that it had for taking the gospel to a whole group of young people who otherwise would not have been reached. But I also knew of the tense relationship that existed before NOS decided to step out on its own. Although I was not pastorally responsible for NOS, I did feel a concern for how they were doing. This concern intensified as I was preaching on the seven churches in Revelation through the summer of 1994.

When we got to Thyatira, I felt as though I had two applications of the message from that passage. One was for St Thomas' and another was disturbingly about the Nine O'Clock Service. I sensed that God was saying that the Nine O'Clock Service had been gripped by the same problems as those present in the church at Thyatira, and that he was working his purposes out to close it down. I told the other members of staff about my feelings on this matter and we decided that we would make this a matter for prayer over the coming weeks and months.

About nine months later, around Easter time, I became convinced that God would soon work out what he had planned for the Nine O'Clock Service and the people within it. I felt sure that we were getting close to the time when he would close it down. I shared this again with the staff, and again we resolved to pray. By the time I had my dream in Greece, I had been in the process of praying and listening to God about NOS for at least a year. Still I had no idea what it was that I should do other than pray.

Much of the shock that we might have experienced was reduced by the fact that we had been talking about this very event for the last year. As we had been praying, we were equipped to make some speedy decisions that helped us in the coming weeks. Because the media were unable to contact most of the leaders of the Nine O'Clock Service, and because the church itself met in a downtown leisure center, there was an immediate call on us to provide shots and pictures of our church where the Nine O'Clock Service had begun, and a call on us to respond to the information-hungry newshounds.

For the next couple of weeks, we were featured on local and national TV and radio, and almost all the leadership team of St Thomas' were interviewed by the major national newspapers. Because we were prepared, this whole process was surprisingly easy and much of the unpleasantness of being under this kind of media spotlight was removed. The people of St Thomas' in the midst of this were encouraged because the staff were able to lead with confidence.

We have of course also had our fair share of public shame and slander through social media.

Envy is always such a powerful mechanism and it is the driving force behind so much of the damage we see done by social media.

JEZEBEL

Some people have asked me since whether I should have gone public with what I felt God was telling me a year before. This is always a difficulty with a spiritual insight. The only answer I have is that I had no peace in sharing these things other than with the other leaders of the church, and that I felt that God had given us the insight so that we could pray.

> *Nevertheless, I have this against you: You tolerate that woman Jezebel, who calls herself a prophetess. By her teaching she misleads my servants into sexual immorality and the eating of food sacrificed to idols*
>
> **Revelation 2:20**

As I prayed, the issue seemed to be focused around the code word Jezebel in the letter to Thyatira. To understand what this means, we need to look at the history of this name. Jezebel was the daughter of the king of Tyre. Like all women in the ancient world, she was devalued and put in a place of subjugation and bondage that offended God's will and crushed her spirit. She was first owned by her father. This alone was enough to devalue her, but it was compounded when she became the property of her husband, Ahab, the King of Israel. Her crushed spirit responded with aggression, rebellion, and a thirst for power that would deliver her from her bondage. She wanted freedom from the oppression she had suffered all her life and the way she could do it was to take the power from the people who had hurt her.

So she grabbed authority wherever she could. In doing this she rejected the divinely appointed authorities in her life. The society of which she was a part did not act justly toward her, and no doubt she resented this, but these imperfect social structures, though not designed by God, could have been used to demonstrate power in the midst of weakness as the Queen of the story did in the book of Ester. Her father, her husband, the social order of which she was a participant, could have been used by God to help and not hinder her. Perhaps understandably, she chose not to submit to any of these authorities, deciding rather to rebel. She rejected their role in her life and at the same time rejected the God who had established them.

Ahab was the other side of the coin. He had probably been indulged all of his life. Any time he wanted anything, he got it. He had been spoiled and had never had to take responsibility for anything. He never had to think about anything too difficult. Everything was done for him, and so he became self-centered and passive, expecting everything to be laid on just for him.

He may have had busy parents who gave him things instead of human affection. This would have confused and injured him when he was a boy. Eventually he grew up to be the King of Israel, still passive, expecting everything to be laid on for him — still ducking responsibility whenever he could.

Sounds like a perfect marriage, doesn't it? A woman who had been crushed in spirit and a man who had been over-indulged all his life. What a partnership — they were made for each other!

Israel had been divided by the time Ahab came to the throne. Seeking the quiet life, Ahab wanted peace with his neighbors. One of them, the king of Tyre, offered a treaty ratified by the marriage between Ahab and Jezebel, and so these two very different individuals came together. Jezebel came and joined Ahab and brought all her gods with her, as was customary at the time. Perhaps he thought it would better express the pluralist society they all lived in, because although Ahab tipped his hat to Yahweh, he was unconcerned that his new bride brought her gods with her.

Now Jezebel's gods, Baal and Ashtoreth, were very successful. Their popularity was built on fairly obvious attractions — wild parties, free sex — all under the guise of a religion sanctioned by the crown.

As well as her gods, Jezebel brought her ambition. She wanted power and could not understand her husband's weakness. In time she grew to despise him and eventually learned to control him and his kingdom. Naboth's vineyard is a good example of this process taking place.

Some time later there was an incident involving a vineyard belonging to Naboth the Jezreelite. The vineyard was in Jezreel, close to the palace of Ahab king of Samaria. Ahab said to Naboth, "Let me have your vineyard to use for a vegetable garden, since it is close to my palace. In exchange I will give you a better vineyard or, if you prefer, I will pay you whatever it is worth."

But Naboth replied, "The Lord forbid that I should give you the inheritance of my fathers" (I Kings 21:1-3).

Naboth's identity was tied up with the things that had been given to him by his ancestors. Giving up the vineyard would be like giving away his name. He could not do that. This was "Naboth's vineyard'" This was his inheritance, his identity.

Enter Jezebel.

> *Jezebel came in and asked him, "Why are you so sullen? Why won't you eat?'*
>
> *He answered her, " Because I said to Naboth the Jezreelite, 'Sell me your vineyard; or if you prefer, I will give you another vineyard in its place.' But he said, 'I will not give you my vineyard.'*
>
> *Jezebel his wife said, "Is this how you act as king over Israel? Get up and eat! Cheer up. I'll get you the vineyard of Naboth the Jezreelite"*
>
> **I Kings 21:5-7**

Jezebel signed a letter in the name of Ahab to the elders of the town where Naboth lived. They got some scoundrels together to accuse Naboth of treason and rebellion against the king, and stoned him to death. Then the leaders of the town contacted Jezebel and said, "Naboth has been stoned and is dead'"(I Kings 21:14).

Jezebel went back to Ahab and said:

> *"Get up and take possession of the vineyard of Naboth the Jezreelite that he refused to sell you. He is no longer alive, but dead."*
>
> **I Kings 21:14-16**

Ahab's weakness and Jezebel's hunger for power put the nation in desperate trouble. God sought to rectify this by sending Elijah, perhaps the most powerful of all the Old Testament prophets. But even though the ministry of Elijah was accompanied by some of the greatest miracles in the Bible, Ahab and Jezebel would not turn to the Lord and give up their idols.

The history of Jezebel and Ahab gives us an insight into the problems that the church in Thyatira faced in the first century.

RIPE FOR DECEPTION

Thyatira probably had the smallest church of the seven. A small place, yet the longest letter and perhaps some of the hardest words in the New Testament. Jesus was very concerned about what he saw in this church. He commended them as always for the things he could praise — their faith, their perseverance, their love. But he also deals very precisely and unequivocally with the problems that he saw. They tolerated something he could not: a person whose ministry was leading the church into sin — he gave her a code name — Jezebel.

The city of Thyatira had many guilds. A guild functioned in the first century rather as unions do today. A god was attached to each guild, and it would be worshipped by the members. The lists of these guilds that have been dug up in the archaeological digs around Thyatira are the longest and most comprehensive found anywhere. Thyatira was a trading post, a stop off point on the way to Pergamum. Here trade was everything. It was like a glorified market, and because of this the trading guilds held sway. There was no other authority that could compete.

The resident population would have been very small and entirely dependent on the passing trade. In a place where trade was so important you would be expected to honor the guilds and their gods. If you had recently become a Christian, it was expected that the guild remained the focus of your life. The problem was that the guild worshipped their own personal gods and not the God of the Bible. At their yearly celebrations and festivals, everything

started well enough, but by the end the members would not
only have entered into idol worship — the recognition of the
guild deities — but also immorality, as so often happened at
pagan festivals. The immorality was sanctioned and given the
official nod of approval because it involved so called "religious"
prostitutes.

If you were a Christian and were part of one of these guilds,
obviously you would feel challenged to leave. But if you left,
where would you get your livelihood? The guilds controlled
everything. They ran the marketplace. How could you get access
to the normal means of trade and exchange? How could you
survive if you were not a member of a guild? Of course, these new
Christians had the teaching of Jesus who had said that God would
take care of all of his children when they were in need, and they
had the example of godly men and women like Joseph, Esther
and Daniel who were able to succeed in a hostile environment.
But still they panicked. They even had the recent example of the
Apostle Paul, who, while pioneering the church in the region,
supported himself as a tentmaker without becoming involved
in the guild worship. But perhaps, understandably, they worried
about their livelihood and before long were ripe for deception.

Into this situation of fear and anxiety came someone who had
spiritual authority within the church — someone who was known
as a prophet. Unfortunately, this prophet had been influenced by
the teachings of the Nicolaitans and therefore brought a message
to the church that led it into spiritual bondage. The message
was that God said it was all right to be a member of a guild. No
doubt the message was couched in a language and style that made
it acceptable. Deception is always close to the truth, otherwise it
would fool no one.

Perhaps the prophetess expressed the message in terms of

evangelism. "Here is our opportunity to really witness to the world by staying involved in the guild and sharing our faith at the same time." Of course, it was not membership of the guild that posed a problem, it was everything that came with it which led these Christians into immorality.

But how did the situation degenerate into this terrible state? The process began with an unchecked, untested message which was assumed to have been from God. Guild membership was therefore endorsed and the members of the church who had received this message got involved with the guild activities. This inevitably led to moral compromise and eventually wholesale sin. Of course, the presence of the Holy Spirit within the believers and their limited knowledge of Scripture would cause their conscience to be pricked, and at this point no doubt they returned to their prophetess for counsel. She may have offered them a message of forgiveness, telling them to be more alert and perhaps encouraging them that things were not as bad as they thought, because God was more interested in their spiritual life than their physical behavior.

This kind of situation requires two types of people — one like Ahab, the other like Jezebel. Of course rather than analyzing others we should first ask whether we have a tendency one way or the other. Do you have a tendency to be an aggressive, rebellious, hurt individual like Jezebel, or a passive, spoilt, injured individual like Ahab? I have encountered both in the church. They are not of course always divided along lines of gender. They can be either male or female. There are **Jeze** Bills as well as Jezebels!

These two personality types are at opposite ends of the spectrum. There is a line or continuum between Ahab and Jezebel, and most people have a tendency toward one end or the other, toward Ahab or his wife.

ESCAPING DECEPTION

Fortunately God always provides the warning signs when we face the crisis of deception: First there is our conscience. We become disturbed by a general lack of peace and an awareness that we may be doing wrong. There is the challenge from others around us who are uncomfortable about our behavior and there is a conviction that comes from hearing the word of God. All of these contribute to producing a change in our lives.

Just at the right time, God reminds us that we are sinners which means we have both a tendency toward sin and an inbuilt desire to cover up our failings.

Health Check Warning Signs

- Conscience — lack of inner peace
- Challenge — friends think you might be doing wrong
- Conviction — God's Word revealing the truth about us and our actions

What Is the solution? On the one hand we have rebellion and power seeking, on the other we have passivity and dodging responsibility. Basically both kinds of people are seeking to serve themselves. But if we are likely to end up one way or the other, what do we need to know?

In his first letter Peter offers a few pointers. To those who want to control situations, take power and manipulate, he says:

Clothe yourselves with humility toward one another because 'God opposes the proud but gives grace to the humble' Humble yourselves therefore under God's mighty hand that he may lift you up in due time. Cast all your anxiety on him because he cares for you.

I Peter 5:5-7

To those looking for the easy option and the quiet life he says:

Be self-controlled and alert. Your enemy the devil prowls around like a roaring lion looking for someone to devour. Resist him, standing firm in the faith because you know that your brothers throughout the world are undergoing the same kind of sufferings.

I Peter 5:8-9

What does the person with a tendency toward rebellion need to hear? They must submit to God. Our submission to God-given authority is submission to God and not to people. Submitting does not mean cringing in the corner, it means recognizing that God is in charge.

Occasionally, those who have been placed in authority over us lose their right to exercise this role in our lives — parents who wilfully abuse their children, husbands who continuously beat their wives, governments that enslave and tyrannize their people. In such circumstances, a person needs to continue to submit to God and actively seek freedom through prayer and action. Submitting to God and listening to him will allow him to provide the rescue that we need. But in most cases when the circumstances are less serious, God will test our faithfulness and determination by saying, Will you submit to the people and the authorities that I have set up?'

You might say, "But they are bad at the job and they have hurt me.' He will say, "But I am good at the job and I didn't hurt you."

Trusting God is the issue. Submission to others flows from trust in him. As we trust, we learn to submit and in our submission we are protected. That is why James says, "Submit yourselves, then, to God Resist the devil, and he will flee from you" (James 4:7). Our submission to God protects us from the enemy. As we trust God we are protected and he begins the healing of the injuries on which our rebellion and anger are built.

And what about those who get trapped in passivity? They need to hear, "Be self-controlled and alert. Your enemy the devil prowls around like a roaring lion looking for someone to devour. Resist him, standing firm in the faith" (I Pet 5:8-9). This does not mean striving and struggling in our own strength, but standing in his strength which comes as we recognize our weakness and rely on him.

In *Pilgrim's Progress*, Christian hears lions roaring on the road ahead of him. He knows that he must go forward but is still afraid. When he gets closer to the lions, he sees they are chained and unable to reach the travelers who stay on the path. So it is with the devil. He cannot reach us if we stay on the path that God has prescribed. We will never know freedom from the fear of the enemy if we are paralyzed by inactivity. We must move on, clinging to the Lord who will hold us in his way and protect us from evil.

INVITATION TO TRUE IDENTITY

Whichever tendency we have, whether toward rebellion or passivity, aggression or responsibility dodging, we need to surrender to the Lord's agenda for our lives and trust him. That is what the church in Thyatira needed to hear. The Lord shocked them into hearing it by hard words that would get their attention.

I can remember a period of hard testing when I felt as though
I was hanging on to God with my fingernails. The easiest path
would have been to surrender to the temptations that I was being
presented with daily and follow my basic human drives. Time and
time again I confessed to the Lord my difficulty in resisting the
temptations, and I asked Christian friends to pray for me. At last,
relief came. A person entirely ignorant of my situation came to
me and said that the Lord had given them a Bible verse . which
they believed was for me. It was from this letter: "To him who
overcomes and does my will to the end . . . I will also give him the
morning star."

Before the first light in the sky, as morning draws near and when
the night is at its darkest, a single bright star appears on the
horizon. The morning star means a fresh start — a new day. That
is precisely what God did. Within a few days, the strength of the
temptation abated, and within a few weeks the whole situation
was completely transformed. I hung on. He protected me and
has since used the new phase "the new day" to bring healing and
restoration in many areas of my life.

The message to Thyatira is a message to us. Don't be manipulated
by Jezebels and get sucked into this worldview. If you hold on,
you'll receive the morning star, the new day. We can trust this
promise based on what we know about the Bible--the twin
themes of Covenant and Kingdom we find throughout the
Bible. Our relationship with God is about these two realities--
the covenant relationship we have with God, and the Kingdom
responsibility we have to rule as God's representative.

When we look at the covenant side, we are reminded that God is
revealed to us as Father. Because He is Father, we have an identity
and identity of nobility and royalty. We have an identity of
security. Someone in Thyatira would embrace this identity instead

of the identity of being in a particular guild. They would not be passive like Ahab, nor would they be angry like Jezebel. When we lean into this true identity, we are able to obey. Obedience comes out of identity.

And because our Father is the King, we have power based on the authority the King gives us. That's what Jesus emphasizes in the final verses of this letter.

To the one who is victorious and does my will to the end, I will give authority over the nations— that one 'will rule them with an iron scepter and will dash them to pieces like pottery'—just as I have received authority from my Father. I will also give that one the morning star.

Jesus is reminding this church that if they hold fast to their covenant identity and their Kingdom responsibility, they will overcome the Ahabs and Jezebels and guilds and their gods and everything around them. The key was understanding and embracing their identity, even though the world invites them to different direction. This reminder is just as important for us.

There is a challenge in this letter for us, of course. If we are like Ahab, God calls us out of our entitled nature. If we are like Jezebel, God calls us to his truth. But the challenge in this letter comes with the empowering, elevating call is to simply live up to all that in God's grace you can live up --which is our identity not as Ahab or Jezebel but as a child of God.

As we take on our true identity, other things begin to happen that we would never imagine, and we begin to see ourselves in a way that perhaps we've never seen ourselves before.

When identity that comes from the Father becomes the leading message in our life, obedience becomes a joyful grace-filled experience, and something remarkable happens. We realize that our Father is the King, and he has given his children authority and power. The Father gives his children their identity, and in this identity we have authority over our circumstances. What great news! We receive the morning star because we are children of the King.

CRISIS AND CULTURAL EARTHQUAKES: CLARITY IN COMMUNITY

The church at Thyatira faced a crisis of deception. When crisis strikes and everything shakes ,we are even more prone to fall victim to this kind of deception. We need clarity that comes from God, and the best way to find this is in community. This is why the writer of Hebrews followed this discussion about shakable and unshakable things with the following.

Keep on loving one another as brothers and sisters. Do not forget to show hospitality to strangers, for by so doing some people have shown hospitality to angels without knowing it. Continue to remember those in prison as if you were together with them in prison, and those who are mistreated as if you yourselves were suffering. Marriage should be honored by all, and the marriage bed kept pure, for God will judge the adulterer and all the sexually immoral. Keep your lives free from the love of money and be content with what you have, because God has said,

> *God has said,*
> > *"Never will I leave you;*
> > *never will I forsake you.*
>
> *So we say with confidence,*
> > *"The Lord is my helper; I will not be afraid*
> > *What can mere mortals do to me?"*

Hebrews 13:5-6

Our natural reaction during crisis is to be self-oriented. Think about how people hoarded toilet paper during the COVID-19 pandemic. This was a self-orientation--someone saying, "I don't care what happens to anyone else. I want to make sure I am taken care of." But this instinct to self-orientation is the opposite of what Scriptures encourage. We are supposed to extend resources to each other and keep loving each other as family.

Just as God wants to make us courageous in crisis, he also wants to make us compassionate. Practicing this kind of care and compassion in our Christian communities reminds us of our identity as God's children and God's representatives, and leads us to extend compassion to everyone--strangers and prisoners and even those who have mistreated us.

HUDDLE STUDY GUIDE

Are you more likely to rebel like Jezebel or to be passive like Ahab? What are the particular dangers you face based on your tendencies?

Why does God give us authority and power? What are we supposed to use these things for?

How have you found greater access to God's power in your life? How can our Huddle help each other do this?

FOR ADDITIONAL REFLECTION

Are you more of an Ahab or a Jezebel? Most of us fall between one extreme or the other. This assessment can give you more insight into your personality. Score yourself on a scale of 1 to 5 on the following statements for both the Jezebel and Ahab reflections below.

JEZEBEL

I see conflict as a means of establishing control in a situation

I try to win the argument so as to gain the upper hand and strengthen my own position

I pick fights

I look for ways of asserting my personality over others

I reject the idea of someone else having authority over me

I am always trying to break free from what I see as other people's dominance over me

I have to respect someone in order to obey them

I say, "I will obey as soon as I find someone to respect and trust"

TOTAL:

If your score is more than 20, it may indicate a tendency toward the Jezebel end of the personality spectrum.

AHAB

I give in whenever I am confronted

I agree with what others say so as to keep the peace

I avoid conflict

My fear of the consequences of conflict (losing face, being exposed, feeling vulnerable) makes me avoid dealing with things, even when they are very pressing or important

I let people push me around

I fail to tell others when they have hurt me because I am afraid of the consequences

I expect other people to make decisions for me, even the big ones that affect the whole of my life

I let others dominate me

TOTAL:

If your score is more than 20, it may indicate a tendency toward the Ahab end of the personality spectrum.

The higher of the two scores represents the greater tendency in your life. For example, if you score 10 for Jezebel and 35 for Ahab you can safely assume that you have a greater tendency toward Ahab's personality type.. Reflect on what you found here, and if you're confused, process it with your Huddle or with other friends to interpret what God is saying to you and what you need to do about it.

5

SARDIS
A CRISIS OF COMPACENCY

To the angel of the church in Sardis write:

These are the words of him who holds the seven spirits of God and the seven stars. I know your deeds; you have a reputation of being alive, but you are dead. Wake up! Strengthen what remains and is about to die, for I have found your deeds unfinished in the sight of my God. Remember, therefore, what you have received and heard; hold it fast, and repent. But if you do not wake up, I will come like a thief, and you will not know at what time I will come to you.

Yet you have a few people in Sardis who have not soiled their clothes. They will walk with me, dressed in white, for they are worthy. The one who is victorious will, like them, be dressed in white. I will never blot out the name of that person from the book of life, but will acknowledge that name before my Father and his angels. Whoever has ears, let them hear what the Spirit says to the churches.

Revelation 3:1-6

Complacency was the problem in Sardis. The church had a great reputation for life, but somehow had become so lax in its spiritual life that Jesus was ready to come as a thief to confront the spiritual decay that had gripped it.

The roots of complacency in Sardis were found in its social history. The church had picked up the spirit of the city in which it was planted and was now suffering the consequences. The Lord knew all about them and their reputation for spiritual life. But far from life, the Lord said that they now were characterized by death.

> *Wake up! Strengthen what remains and is about to die, for I have not found your deeds complete in the sight of my God.*

Revelation 3:2

How had a church with so much potential come to such a state?

In 549 BC Sardis was capital of the Lydian Empire. In the citadel of Sardis, Croesus, King of Lydia, felt confident and secure. From his palace high up in his fortress city he could see for miles. He could see the northern hills beyond the broad plain of the Hermus Valley. He could trace the path of the Hermus River as it meandered its way to Smyrna and the western sea.

But it was not the beauty of his surroundings that engaged him on this occasion. He was interested in something else — the deployment of the Persian army as it began to make camp all around the acropolis on which his city was built. The tents and campfires, men and horses, pennants and banners of this new and dangerous foe were all clearly visible. Cyrus, King of Persia, was tightening a stranglehold around his city.

Croesus decided to wait it out. That upstart Cyrus, self-proclaimed "King of the Medes," was not going to force him into any hasty action. He would wait. It was unnecessary and dangerous to engage his enemy outside the city gates. The same result could be achieved by waiting. Cyrus could not win, for Sardis was completely impregnable! The only point of access was the southern gate built on a low narrow shoulder of land at the southern end of the plateau on which his city was built. But this was heavily fortified and guarded by a large contingent of his men. Even if Cyrus chose to attack with his best men, he would be easily repulsed. Cyrus and his army would soon tire of waiting, especially as the impossibility of victory set in. They would go and look for easier prizes, and Croesus and his people would go on with their lives. In the unlikely event that a stalemate was reached, he knew he could rely on his wealth to buy off Cyrus and sue for peace. What great satisfaction there must have been in knowing he could always fall back on his royal treasury — perhaps the largest and richest in the world — to get him out of trouble.

On the plain below Cyrus had different plans. He did not have stalemate in mind. He was going to defeat Croesus and plunder his fabled treasury and use his gold to finance his plans to create the greatest empire the world had ever seen. He had already dealt with Astyages, his maternal grandfather, and taken his crown as King of the Medes. Now came Croesus — the next on his list of the Old Guard kings. After Croesus he would take Assyria and eventually the ultimate prize — Babylon. His plans could not allow Croesus to remain undefeated or his impregnable fortress city of Sardis to remain intact; Cyrus had to take it, and he would.

He had sent out a reconnaissance mission and it had already returned with some important information. The sheer — almost vertical — rock face of the acropolis was, as expected, unscalable, except for one place. The perpendicular cliffs that surrounded the citadel were split by a huge crack (what modern-day mountaineers call a chimney). This crack extended from the bottom to the top of the plateau and offered a skilful climber a slim but nevertheless real chance of scaling it. The rock itself was crumbling and treacherous. But with daggers pushed into the cracks for foot and hand holds, and ropes secured at the top for others to follow, an attack under the cloak of darkness might be possible. Cyrus decided to take the chance and so the men were selected and briefed, the preparations made, and the night chosen for the assault.

Back inside Sardis a general air of confidence, engendered no doubt by the King's own lack of concern, pervaded the atmosphere. This confidence was already beginning to give way to complacency. Cyrus' plans had obviously stalled, and they expected to hear any day that the Persians had left or were seeking terms of peace. While they were waiting, they might as well relax. Perhaps this was the reason that guards could no longer be found at their posts. Laxity — something for which the people of Sardis were known — was creeping in everywhere.

Sardis fell to Cyrus during the night. His special forces climbed the cliffs and found the walls unguarded and unprotected. Many of the defenders were killed as they slept. While Sardis snored, the Persians attacked. Cyrus took the city, plundered the treasury, annexed the Kingdom of Lydia and then turned his sights on Assyria and Babylon.

Cyrus became a great and a good emperor, spoken of in Scripture as Israel's anointed deliverer, and instrument of divine sovereignty (see Isaiah 44:28). He returned the Jews and all the exiled peoples to their homelands and provided funds for rebuilding their places of worship, including the temple in Jerusalem. Croesus became a minor figure in history remembered only for his untold riches. "He's as rich as Croesus," the expression went, but few could remember who Croesus was, or what he had done.

Having fallen to Cyrus, Sardis eventually recovered and grew again to a position of prominence and wealth within the region of Asia Minor. When Antiochus the Great threatened the city in 218 BC, it should have learned its lesson. But fell in exactly the same way as before. Antiochus, learning from Cyrus' success, used the same strategy to defeat the city. Again the attackers climbed the acropolis at night. Again the walls were unguarded, and again the city fell.

In time the city again recovered, and again the same old problem returned. There were other warnings about complacency, like the earthquake of AD 17, but by the time John recorded the words of the risen Lord, the city and the church had fallen victim to the crisis of complacency again. The disease was not only serious — it was terminal! Today the city of Sardis no longer exists and neither does the church!

COMPLACENCY

> *Wake up! Strengthen what remains and is about to die, for I have not found your deeds complete in the sight of my God. Remember, therefore, what you have received and heard; obey it, and repent. But if you do not wake up, I will come like a thief and you will not know at what time I will come to you.*

Revelation 3:2-3

Complacency was so ingrained in the character of the people of Sardis that the church itself displayed many of the same characteristics that had historically been part of the people around them. Throughout its history, Sardis had one warning after another about its complacent attitude and about the dangers of wealth and indiscipline. Now the church needed to learn the same lessons.

On December 7, 1941, Commander Mitsuo Fuchida watched the sun rise as he flew his bomber over the north Pacific. The blue skies and first rays of the rising sun — symbol of the Japanese imperial navy — seemed to augur well for his mission. His task was to lead the attack on the US fleet at anchor in Pearl Harbour.

He waited to be sure of his target. There it was — 'the tiger and her cubs' — just as Admiral Yamamoto had predicted, asleep and unprepared. Now came the hour of reckoning. All the planning and preparation, all the practice and training, would result either in victory or defeat.

In fact, the situation was better than he could have hoped. The defenses were at a very low state of readiness. The guns protecting the harbor were unmanned. The planes were sitting targets on the runways. Although the US had accurate intelligence of the aggressive intentions of the Japanese, having broken their secret codes some months earlier, there was still no preparation. Not even a reconnaissance flight had been sent.

Fuchida broke radio silence and signalled the beginning of the attack. Tiger! Tiger! Tiger! (Tora! Tora! Tora! In Japanese) — the attack had begun. From now on the United States and Japan would be locked in mortal conflict until the victor stood triumphant over the Pacific.

The first five minutes of the attack did most of the damage. By the time the attack was over and Fuchida was leading his virtually unscathed force back to the aircraft carriers waiting in the north Pacific. Pearl Harbour and the US Fleet had been almost completely destroyed. Of the eight US battleships in the harbor, three were sunk, with one capsized and four seriously damaged. Three light cruisers and three destroyers were sunk, and 261 planes were destroyed with many others damaged. Of the service personnel, 3226 were dead and 1272 wounded. The Japanese lost only twenty-nine of their 360 planes.

Vice Admiral Chuichi Nagumo, commander of the Pearl Harbor offensive, could hardly believe his good fortune. As the reports came in, they exceeded his wildest dreams. But it was not until the final report that he realized he had missed his main target. The three key US aircraft carriers were out on maneuvers, and had for that reason avoided the attack. Nagumo decided, for some reason, not to send the planned second attack. Perhaps he did not want to try his luck again, or perhaps he expected the Americans to counter-attack — no one really knows. The effect was to allow the now helpless defending forces at Pearl Harbor to avoid a complete rout. It also ensured that the oil storage bunkers, sitting unprotected some distance outside Pearl Harbor, were not hit.

These facts would later prove decisive factors in the outcome of the Second World War. The US Pacific fleet had the opportunity to rebuild, refit and engage the enemy within six months. The miraculous victory at Midway, which accounted for the sinking of the Japanese carrier fleet, was directly attributable to Nagumo's failure to send a second attack.

When hearing the reports of success, Admiral Yamamoto, Japan's greatest military mind and architect of the Pearl Harbor strategy, is reported to have said, 'I fear we have awakened a sleeping giant.' His words proved prophetic. Pearl Harbor was a wake-up call to the United States of America. The US campaign finally resulted in the defeat and total capitulation of the Japanese

Emperor and High Command aboard the battleship Missouri in Tokyo Bay. Commander Mitsuo Fuchida was aboard the USS Missouri the day the Emperor surrendered, and was one of the few witnesses to the beginning and the end of the war in the Pacific. After the war he was converted to Christ and became an evangelist working both in Japan and around the world.

The attitude of those who lived in the 'impregnable' Sardis was like that of the officers and men at Pearl Harbor. Complacency had grown to the extent that normal precautions were not taken. Once present this attitude is remarkably persistent and infectious.

Complacency is a deadly spiritual disease which will result in tragedy if left unchecked. The problem is, that if the conditions are right, the disease returns. It will develop wherever a community becomes self-serving. The United States, like Sardis, has been infected by complacency and this has affected both the church and the nation as a whole.

A similar though less obvious situation persisted in Europe during World War II. Germany was able to attack and conquer much of Europe because of the lack of preparation and forethought among the leaders of the western powers. These leaders are characterized by Neville Chamberlain waving his piece of paper on which Adolf Hitler had signaled his agreement to peaceful coexistence. He returned declaring "peace in our time." What followed is well documented. Europe quickly fell to German invasion forces and only Britain remained to resist the spread of this unprecedented evil.

In Britain the celebrations of victory at the end of the Second World War gave way to feelings of self-satisfaction and a lack of national resolve. Many who lived through those times recall a common desire to leave the old world behind. The problem was that in leaving the old world behind, they also left the morality and values that made the nation great. In little more than a decade, the national spirit had declined and the generation of the swinging sixties was born. While other nations — not least among them Germany—rebuilt and restructured, Britain, having won the war in Europe, now began to wage war on itself. The record of the last fifty years is one littered with social and political conflict and division. Lurching from left to right, from social contract to social conflict, Britain has hardly known peace since the war was won. It would seem that the growing complacency in each generation since the war has given birth to greater apathy in the next and this prevailing spirit has infected the church.

Millions of people have left the church, and although the exodus appears to be slowing down, still hundreds leave or die every week and remain unreplaced. The English church census records some hopeful signs in some denominations, particularly the newer types of church networks, but still we are losing hundreds of people a week. We all know it is true, and yet little changes. Overall Christianity in Britain is marked by death rather than by life. "Wake up! Strengthen what remains and is about to die, for I have not found your deeds complete in the sight of my God' (Rev:3.2).

How do we avoid the pitfalls and learn the lessons? We need to listen to Jesus. He has a lot to say about complacency.

CAUSE AND EFFECT
In the parable of the rich man, Jesus reveals the causes and the dangers of complacency:

> *The ground of a certain rich man produced a good crop.*
> *He thought to himself 'What shall I do? I have no place*
> *to store my crops.'*

Then he said, 'This is what I'll do. I will tear down my barns and build bigger ones, and there I will store all my grain and my goods. And I'll say to myself "You have plenty of good things laid up for many years. Take life easy; eat, drink and be merry"'

But God said to him, 'You fool! This very night your life will be demanded from you. Then who will get what you have prepared for yourself?'

This is how it will be with anyone who stores up things for himself but is not rich toward God .

Luke 12:16-21

The rich man's problem was that he did not understand that it was God who had given him his fields, blessed him and made him wealthy. His success was nothing to do with being a self-made man. The parable warns us to guard our lives against the deadly effects of pride. In the parable the story shows a man saying, "Look what I've achieved." And God responded, "This very night your life will be demanded from you." The man's pride led to self-reliance. Self-reliance led to laziness. Laziness led to complacency. Complacency led to death.

On another occasion Jesus addresses believers who think their activities will somehow impress him. Even healing the sick, casting out demons, preaching the gospel are not the credentials that Jesus is looking for in his followers. He is seeking a relationship. To everyone who does not have that relationship, he says, "I never knew you" (Matthew 7:23).

We can allow all our doing to overtake our being. Many of us would be better described as human doings rather than human beings. Instead of being with Jesus and allowing our relationship with him to take priority, we focus on doing things for him. We must remember that Jesus is looking for a friendship first, which means that we must develop that relationship before we do anything else.

THE HOLDER OF LIFE

In the letter to Sardis the ascended Jesus is described as holding the seven spirits of God. This picture is universally interpreted as the risen Lord being able to despatch and pour out the Holy Spirit wherever he wishes. Jesus in effect is saying to the church in Sardis, "I dispense the life of God, but you're as good as dead!"

What is our response? We might think the best thing to do is to run around for a little longer like headless chickens looking as though we are alive, but this is the wrong response! The right response is to come to the one who holds life, who holds the sevenfold Spirit of God, and ask him for life.

In the parable of the ten young girls, five were foolish and five were wise. They all had the right credentials, they were young girls, ready to meet the bridegroom. They all had the right equipment: the lamps, the wicks, and the veils. All knew that the bridegroom would come but only half of them were prepared. They trimmed their lamps and filled them with oil. When the bridegroom took a long time in-coming, those who had prepared were ready for his arrival. The wise girls had brought extra oil just in case they had a long wait. The foolish ones brought only what their lamps would hold and so were not ready. Like the girls in this parable, we cannot make light on our own--we need the fuel of the Holy Spirit. The Holy Spirit is the life we need to draw on continuously as we await the Lord's return. We cannot rely on anything else.

In another parable a rich man thought that he was the reason for all his success and so became self-reliant. In this passage Jesus makes it clear that being in relationship with him is more important than doing something for God. In the story of the ten young girls, we see the dangers of not being prepared.

EFFECTS OF COMPLACENCY

The church in Sardis was proud, inactive and unprepared and was in danger from the very one they thought they served. Complacent attitudes develop when we are proud. Pride leads us to focus on ourselves, our own achievements, and what we have done. The focus becomes doing rather than being. The seeds of pride often grow into lax behaviour and bear fruit in the crises created by poor discipline and preparation.

Are you complacent? Has your life as a Christian bred in you a self-satisfied, slothful, slack and lazy spirit? Are you making the right plans for your life? What can you do if you notice the dangerous signs of complacency in your own life? What are some of the signs that spiritual complacency has begun to affect our spiritual well-being?

Complacency is often created by self-reliance. When we become self-reliant, we trust ourselves more than we trust the Lord. This attitude repels the Spirit of God within us. He is less able to work in and through us because we are not allowing him to do this. One of the immediate consequences of this is that the confidence in God which the Spirit brings begins to ebb away.

This lack of confidence produces a kind of fear which is only removed when we surrender to the work of the Holy Spirit in our hearts.

> *For you did not receive a Spirit that makes you a slave again to fear, but you received the Spirit of sonship. And*

by him we cry, "Abba" Father. The Spirit himself testifies
with our spirit that we are God's children

Romans 8:15-17

We have nothing to fear if we know we are God's children. How
will we know that we lack assurance of salvation? We hope we
have done everything we need to do but we are not sure because
we are focusing on what we have done, rather than the Lord
himself. If we are relying on ourselves, we will lack assurance
because only God can give assurance and we receive it only when
we focus on him. We will find ourselves raking over things that
we have done wrong and presenting them to God for forgiveness
again. God has already declared his forgiveness over our past
sins, but when we look at them we cannot believe that God has
forgiven all this sin and so we decide to ask for forgiveness all over
again.

If we confess our sins, he is faithful and just and will
forgive us our sins and purify us from all unrighteousness.

1 John 1:9

Sometimes the self-reliance that leads to this kind of complacency
is not only expressed in us looking to ourselves but also in looking
to other human beings like our spouse, our friends, or our
ministers. When we fail to look to the Lord, we will always find
someone else to replace him. This can lead to all kinds of dangers,
not least of which is a 'cult' following of powerful and talented
leaders.

On the more mundane level, people who get themselves trapped
into this way of thinking either idolize or criticize their leaders.
They idolize them because they get fed every week, or they
criticize them because they do not. What we need to do is to go

to Jesus who holds the seven stars, which probably means the leaders of our churches, and ask him to feed our leaders. If in the process of going to him, we get fed through others, we will still recognize that it is the Lord who feeds us.

However the most common result of complacency in our lives is a lack of action. We do not respond to the needs of others. We fail to take the opportunities we are offered to serve others and share our faith, and a spiritual sleepiness creeps over us and our church. Are any of these signs of complacency found in your life?

> *Remember, therefore, what you have received and heard;*
> *obey it, and repent.*

Revelation 3:3

If these things are present we need to go to Jesus and confess to him how our complacent attitude has affected us. When we do this, his promise is to forgive, renew, and restore us. Jesus loves us, and his greatest desire is to bless us. But if we do not repent of our complacency the consequences are dire.

> *But if you-do not wake up, I will come like a thief and*
> *you will not know at what time I will come to you.*

Revelation 3:3

As with some of the other churches the risen Lord brings a warning and a promise. The warning and promise relate both to a present-day divine visitation and the Second Coming. At the end of time, Jesus will return like a thief in the night. Between now and then he will at times visit us like a thief. He does this so that his visitations can prepare us for his Second Coming. When he visits us, he removes the props and crutches that we rely on which prevent us from trusting fully in him. Jesus wants to help us grow and mature. To do this he has to remove the props which give us our security and cause us to depend on ourselves.

We may think this is uncharacteristic of the Jesus we have come to know. But he does it. And he does it because he loves us. He knows that our happiness and peace depend on him. He knows that if we rely on anyone or anything more than him we will suffer, and so he removes the props and crutches, even the ones we hold most dear.

I have a tendency toward self-reliance. But over the years, God has shaken or removed many of my props and crutches. The insecurity that comes from depending on myself and my own ability has been replaced by the peace and security of knowing that he is in charge. It is a little bit like the game KerPlunk! This children's game has a transparent cylinder containing marbles held in place by thin plastic straws which criss-cross through the cylinder into holes. As the straws are removed by each player in turn, the marbles become more and more liable to fall. In time, the marbles begin to drop, at first in ones and twos and then in larger numbers. Eventually, the unfortunate player who removes the last vital straw finds that he has more marbles than anybody else and is out!

I have been through times when it seemed as though God had removed all the straws and my whole life seemed to fall in a great heap on the floor. These have proved to be particularly helpful experiences which have caused me to trust God more and allow his grace to break into my life. It seems as though now I have to be aware of only one or two marbles falling before I run back to him and confess my self-reliance and surrender control to him again.

PREPARED FOR LIFE

This life is a preparation for the life to come. An opportunity to build into our life things that will last. When God visits us, he does so to prepare us for heaven so that he might purify us here and save us from the judgement to come. His visitation will reveal the things that will be consumed in the end anyway. The best thing to do is to let go. Why hang on to the things that will be consumed? Why cling to the things that are being prepared for the fire?

Jesus will visit us in this way and will continue until we hold on to him alone. He does this because he loves us and wants us to cling to him. Real security is only found in Jesus and sometimes he will shake our false security in other things so that we cry out and run to him. Then when he blesses us with material things we will not cling to them or find our security in them but will gladly share them and see them as a benefit for others as well as for ourselves. He gives that we might receive the gifts and pass them on.

The idea of visitation includes the concept of inspection. The original Greek word used by Luke in his account of Jesus weeping over Jerusalem is the same word that underlies the role of a bishop who comes to oversee and inspect God's work in the congregation. Surely the coronavirus has been a period when Jesus has come to inspect his church and some of been found wanting. Many churches who had been given the opportunity to develop missional communities and house churches in the years before the pandemic chose not to -- all for various reasons. They preferred the old way rather than a new and ancient pattern of the New Testament household. The churches that integrated missional communities, house churches, or families on mission as a central element of the community life testify to having done really well during the pandemic compared to other churches that did not.

What is God saying to you and your congregation that he will later come to visit you about? Are there things that he's teaching you now that later he will want to inspect during a time of divine visitation?

But there is another side to all of this. Visitation need not mean only discipline and chastisement. It also means victory and celebration. In the same way divine visitation prepares us for judgement, it also prepares us for eternal celebration. God's intention is to wake his complacent Sleeping Beauty, dress her in the white robes of victory, and celebrate with her the arrival of his kingdom. That is what the last words of this letter are all about.

> *He who overcomes will, like them, be dressed in white I will never blot out his name from the book of life, but will acknowledge his name before my Father and his angels. He who has an ear, let him hear what the Spirit says to the churches*

Revelation 3:5-6

We have a dangerous, even deadly, tendency toward complacency as a society and as a church, but God's desire is to wake us and bless us and remove from us the soiled clothes of slothfulness and bedeck us with the finery of the kingdom. In his patience and generosity God desires to stir us from our sleep and wake us up to all that he has for us.

CRISIS AND CULTURAL EARTHQUAKES: NOT COMPLACENCY BUT CULTURAL INTELLIGENCE

In the United States, one of the main things that made people leave COVID-19 quarantines after two months was nationwide protests about racism and police brutality against minorities. What shook people out of complacency so violently that they were willing to risk becoming infected with coronavirus? It was that they became aware of and intelligent about a cultural issue in a way they had not been before.

When everything is shaken by crisis, we have seen that God leads us to courage and to compassion and to community. As we engage in community with other Christians, and as we show compassion to strangers and prisoners and even our enemies, we discover a longing around us for cultural intelligence.

Too often, those of us with privilege (I put myself in this category) have a mind-set that causes bias toward people who are not privileged like us. But we need a different mind-set. We need cultural intelligence about what is really going on around us. With courage and compassion and community and cultural intelligence, we can begin to share the connecting story that links all of us to God, and in doing so help everyone discover their God-given identity and God-given authority.

As we spend time with Jesus in times of retreat (even forced retreat), Jesus will speak to us, giving us insight in the culture around us.

HUDDLE STUDY GUIDE

When are you most tempted to be complacent? Why is this a problem?

How do you recognize complacency in the first place?

How does holding on to Jesus lead us out of complacency? What does Jesus lead us to do?

Why does Jesus lead us to victory instead of complacent? Why does he do this for us? What does this victory look like? How does this victory impact the people around us?

FOR ADDITIONAL REFLECTION

Revival is now known by different terms around the world. Whatever the name it is a reviving of God's people by the spirit of God, by the mercy of God, by the grace of God. Sometimes it's called a visitation. Sometimes it's called renewal. Sometimes it's called restoration. In America, uniquely throughout all of Christian history, revival is called awakening.

The first great awakening happened at the end of the 18th century, stirring the hearts of the people in such a way that eventually led to freedom and independence. The second great awakening saw the emergence of great movements amongst African-American people in the early part of the 19th century. The third great awakening took the church from the 19th century into the 20th century in America.

The fact that revival is called awakening reminds us that we so often fall asleep. Something about security, our self-reliance, and our success lulls us to sleep.

That begs a question: Where do you need to wake up today? What do you need to wake up personally? Where does your family need to wake up?

Where are the lost? Where are the young? Where are the disenfranchised and the marginalized? Where are they? Do you see them? If you don't see them, it's because your eyes are closed, and that can only mean that you're dead or asleep. Jesus graciously challenges us to wake up. So reflect and allow Jesus to speak to you about how he wants you to wake up. After you reflect, discuss this with your Huddle or other friends to discern what God is saying and what you need to do about it.

6

PHILADELPHIA
A CRISIS OF EXCOMMUNICATION

To the angel of the church in Philadelphia write:

These are the words of him who is holy and true, who holds the key of David. What he opens no one can shut, and what he shuts no one can open. I know your deeds. See, I have placed before you an open door that no one can shut. I know that you have little strength, yet you have kept my word and have not denied my name. I will make those who are of the synagogue of Satan, who claim to be Jews though they are not, but are liars—I will make them come and fall down at your feet and acknowledge that I have loved you. Since you have kept my command to endure patiently, I will also keep you from the hour of trial that is going to come on the whole world to test the inhabitants of the earth.

I am coming soon. Hold on to what you have, so that no one will take your crown. The one who is victorious I will make a pillar in the temple of my God. Never again will they leave it. I will write on them the name of my God and the name of the city of my God, the new

Jerusalem, which is coming down out of heaven from my God; and I will also write on them my new name. Whoever has ears, let them hear what the Spirit says to the churches.

Revelation 3:7-13

On September 16, 1893, 100,000 people came to a starting line that stretched for miles across the Oklahoma plains. The place was the Cherokee Outlet, east of what is now known as the Oklahoma Panhandle. The time was just before noon. They were waiting for the signal to start them on one of the most remarkable races in human history. All of them hoped to claim one of 42,000 plots of land made available by the US Federal Government. They all knew that many would be disappointed as the fittest and the fastest left them behind. But the prize of 160 acres of virgin farmland, cheap and ready to be settled, was worth the risk.

For those taking part the race represented a great opportunity. Many had started life in poverty and oppression in Europe. Having made their way through New York and the cities of the Eastern seaboard, they were now hoping for a new life of liberty and self-determination on the plains of Oklahoma. This was their way out, their door to a fresh start and a new life.

Poverty and oppression were common among the Christians Jesus addressed in the small city of Philadelphia in Asia Minor. They had remained faithful to their call. Now the risen Lord Jesus was offering them an open door — a way out from the situation that had placed them under so much pressure and a way into something new. These Christians had been excommunicated from the synagogue and prevented from entering into the life of their city as normal citizens. Their faith had brought poverty and need. To these believers who had been locked out from everything, Jesus said that he held the keys that allowed him to open and close whatever he wanted to, and that he had opened a door for them.

OPEN DOORS IN PHILADELPHIA

What does the open door indicate? To the readers it was very clear. Both as residents of this city and as first-century Christians, they understood what Jesus was saying. Philadelphia was the most easterly of the seven cities addressed in Revelation. Philadelphia means brotherly love. It wasn't built — unlike the city in the United States called Philadelphia — on the basis that this would be a place of great brotherly love, but was established by a person of that name. One of the kings of the Attalids during the second century BC, (Attelus Philadelphus II of Pergamum) named the city after himself. It was founded as a frontier post for his kingdom. The Attalids had embraced the Hellenistic way of life. They intended to bring the cultures of Greece and Rome to the peoples of the East. Philadelphia was built as a missionary station for the Greco-Roman culture — it was called the Gateway to the East. It was a transition point, a place of opportunity.

St Louis, Missouri was called the Gateway to the West during the westward expansion of the United States of America. The participants in the Cherokee Outlet landrush probably passed through St Louis on their way to Oklahoma. Keeping this tradition alive, the people of St Louis built a huge arch to symbolize for all time its role in the life and development of the USA. Philadelphia in Asia Minor would have had a similar arch if they could have built it.

The Christians in Philadelphia knew that Jesus was alluding to their past to give them hope for the future, but because they were Christians the symbol of an open door would have been richer still. The New Testament is very clear about the image of the doorway. The fundamental meaning that is used in the apostolic language is of an opportunity to share the gospel with others.

PIONEERS AND SETTLERS AT THE FRONTIER

When the cannon sounded at the Cherokee Outlet, everything would have been dust and noise. If preparations had not been properly made, it would now be too late. The horses and mules, people and wagons roared off, rushing headlong into the plains. As the dust settled and the air cleared, heartbreak was already evident. Hopes for some were already disappearing. Horses had pulled up lame, wagon wheels and axles had collapsed; people both young and old had fallen; provisions and possessions lay strewn all over the ground. But the first to fall were not the only ones to meet disaster that day. Accidents and injury claimed many along the way; argument and strife claimed others at their destination. For those able to stake a claim by driving their wooden peg into the ground, however, this was a glorious day! A day when a new life began on the frontier, when visions and dreams became a reality.

For the families taking part in this race, two achievements were necessary for long-term success. The first was to win the race and get to a plot of land as quickly as possible. The second was surviving there long enough to get through the first harvest. This required two very different kinds of talent and two very different kinds of preparation. The first required the skills and training of an athlete and soldier, the second the builder and farmer.

Success or failure was settled before the cannon was fired. Those who understood the complexities of the situation and prepared for them did well. This also would have been true for the Christians in Philadelphia. If they had learned from their experience and allowed their testing to be the preparation that God wanted it to be, they would be ready to reach the new frontier that God was giving them.

This is also true of us. There is always an open door into some life, some group or community. Our problem is that very often we do not see it. But if we do, there are two things we need. The first is to get to the frontier. The second is to stay there. For this we need everyone involved in the project. No one can be spared. No one is expendable.

Philadelphia was being called to a new frontier for the gospel. Many of us are likewise being called. To ensure that all are included and involved we need to function in our God-given strengths and callings. Some will be good at getting us to the frontier; others will be good at keeping us there. Some are pioneers; others are settlers. Pioneers get us there. Settlers keep us there.

A pioneer is a person who is committed to change, flexibility and speed of operation. A settler is someone who emphasizes order, consistency and stability. One rallies to the idea of doing something new and the other to tending what has already been created. If both groups can work together, we are much more likely to see success both in the short and the long term. However, this is easier said than done. The strengths of one group tend to be the weaknesses of the other, and this can lead to communication problems and other kinds of tensions.

Church leaders can add to the problem by valuing one role more than the other, usually because they belong to that group and see the members of the other group as trouble. This, along with the obvious difficulties in communication between the two groups, has led some churches to be more welcoming to one kind of person than the other. Most churches have both groups present, but some seem to develop a deliberate policy of excluding one or the other. At its worst this process degenerates into an unhealthy situation. We either get the lifeless ghetto of the settler church or the lunatic fringe of the pioneer church. In either case, one group gains ascendancy and drives the others off. Church splits often take place when the natural tensions between these two groups escalate into open acrimony.

All churches need both groups to reach the frontier and stay there. The pioneers have been given by God to help us reach out and initiate new things and the settlers have been given to help us establish what has been found and settle the church into the new pattern of life.

In preparing the church to move, change, and grow, these two groups need to be recognized, valued, and released. Of course, simply identifying these groups, declaring their presence and welcoming their contribution can be an enormous release in itself, because It is great to know that we belong. It is even better to know that we are part of God's resources for the church to achieve its calling.

As these two groups fill the roles they are called to occupy, the church begins to move with the energy that God provides. The pioneers are like the horse pulling the cart. The settlers are the cart following the horse. Church leaders hold the reins and maintain the harness to ensure that both the horse and the cart get to the destination. A horse without a cart can carry only very little, and a cart without a horse can travel only very slowly. We need both.

Are you a pioneer or a settler?

PIONEER  SETTLER

Where are you on this line? All of us are somewhere. At different periods of our life we may move toward the settler end of the line as we get older or have children. We may move toward the pioneer end after the death of a spouse or as we reach retirement. In general however, we are attracted toward one direction or the other and therefore see ourselves as part of one or other of the groups.

There may be a connection between whether we are pioneers or settlers and what kind of ministry we are called to fulfil within the church. Paul makes it clear that everyone in the church operates in one of the fivefold ministries of apostle, prophet, evangelist, shepherd, and teacher.

> But to each one of us grace has been given as Christ apportioned it. It was he who gave some to be apostles, some to be prophets, some to be evangelists, and some to be pastors and teachers

Ephesians 4:7, 11

The closer you get to apostolic kinds of ministry involving such things as church planting and ground-breaking evangelism, the closer you get to the pioneers. The closer you get to pastors and shepherds, who water what is planted, the closer you get to the settlers. By arranging ministries on the pioneer/settler continuum, we can more easily define the ministry to which we are called.

This is of enormous help in discerning God's will for our lives. Incidentally, there are many more settlers in most churches than pioneers.

Some may have problems with this kind of analysis because they assume that such things as apostles no longer exist in the church. Of course, at one level this is correct. There are no apostles like

Jesus, "the apostle and high priest whom we confess" (Hebrews 3:1). There are only twelve apostles of the Lord who sit in judgement on the twelve tribes of Israel. The apostles given the responsibility for setting down the New Testament died out with the close of the canon of Scripture.

But surely there is still apostolic ministry today. Apostle simply means one who is sent out, and of course there are still these kinds of apostles today. Although we do not need any more Scripture, we still need apostles who are sent out to initiate new things for God and his people. No one would doubt that we need to continue to send missionaries out into the field — these are modern-day apostles. No one would doubt the need to establish new churches and new ways of reaching the non-Christian world — we need pioneering apostles for all of this.

MISSION ON THE FRONTIER

After facing the crisis of excommunication, the church in Philadelphia was called to be a missionary church. It was called to go through the open door of God's evangelistic opportunity. As we have seen, these Christians would have understood the image of a door from their own history, but it was also part of the language of mission. Paul used this same image. When writing to the Corinthians he explained his reasons for staying on in Ephesus by saying, "A great door for effective work has opened to me" (I Corinthians 16:9).

Also, when Paul and Barnabas returned from their first missionary journey, Luke records that:

> *They gathered the church together and reported all that God had done through them and how he had opened the door of faith to the Gentiles.*

Acts 14:27

The Christians in Philadelphia would have been familiar with this kind of language and would have understood Jesus to be saying that he was opening a door into witness and missionary activity. To take advantage of this opportunity, they would need to get ready. To do this they would first need to understand that their testing and trials were the preparation that God had allowed to equip them for this opportunity.

Whether we are pioneers or settlers, we are all called to witness. When Jesus sent the Holy Spirit on the day of Pentecost he said to his disciples, "You will receive power when the Holy Spirit comes on you; and you will be my witnesses in Jerusalem, and in all Judea and Samaria, and to the ends of the earth" (Acts 1:8).

Pentecost came and empowered the disciples for witness. There was an open door and many thousands heard the good news and responded.

Has God opened a door for witness to you? God eventually opened a door of witness for me to my family, but I waited years to see my parents become Christians. We were brought up in a happy, pagan family. No one knew God. When I became a Christian at the age of sixteen, I wanted them all to know the gospel and all become Christians right there and then. Eventually my Dad took me on one side and said, "Son, we're getting tired of it, so why don't you just give us a break, and let us off the hook for a while!"

I went away deflated; not knowing what to do. The door to my family was not yet open. I would have to wait for the right time. So I prayed every day, and some years later I found myself standing with my parents in the large baptistry of Ansdell Baptist Church. I had to wait, and the waiting made a more effective witness out of me.

When the door opened, God brought all the circumstances together to make my parents open to the gospel. But still other doors were closed. Sally's father and mother seemed to make no response, even though we prayed for them as well. But over time we both saw a gradual softening. David, Sally's father, seemed to become more open to the idea that he needed God in his life. Experiencing unemployment and illness shook his self-confidence and drew him closer to God. The process seemed quite slow, but when he came to a decision, it all happened very suddenly.

A friend of mine was traveling with me through Manchester, and we stopped off at David and Betty's house on the way, as my friend had accidentally left a magazine in their home. It was not one of those "'creepy Christian" accidents where we accidentally on purpose left a religious tract under the pillow, but a genuine oversight. Satisfying his curiosity, David flipped the magazine until he came to one of the headlines which included the phrase "finding God." At that moment the door opened. When I returned home the next day, David called me. I could hardly make out what he was saying because of the tears. Through the sobs, he asked "How can I find God?"

This was the moment that Sally and I had waited almost twenty years for, an open door to share the gospel at a time when Sally's father was ready to hear and respond. I stepped over the threshold and talked through with him what was happening. What I tried to say was that God had brought him to this point and now wanted to enter his life and bring the change and newness that David so desired. That evening, I wrote to David and encouraged him to open his life to the Lord Jesus so that he could come in and show him all that he had done for him. David and Betty very soon joined their local church and enrolled in the Christian Basics Course. They have never looked back.

In fact, years later, we ran into an old friend of ours who has the largest inner-city youth ministry of Europe. He told us of how he was struggling at the beginning of this ministry so much that he didn't know how they would pay the bills. Then he met this old man who gave him such vital wisdom that it changed the trajectory of that ministry. Turns out that man was Sally's dad, who had been a Christian for only a year or so at the time. God had his purpose, and the door was open in his time. It took a long time, but David became a Christian in plenty of time to help contribute to this ministry.

It may be that you are praying for your family and friends now We can sometimes try to force the doors open, but if the door is shut, leave it shut and wait for Jesus to open it. He holds the keys. Look for open doors and when you see them, go through.

FAITHFULNESS

We know that only God can open the door. So what can we do to prepare? Philadelphia was a faithful church, a church marked by loyalty to Jesus and to one another. Faithful Christians are the ones that God is most able to use. God helped Sally and me to stay faithful in prayer for our parents so that when the door was open, we were ready to go through. Jesus is looking for people who stay close to him, who are not drawn after the next big thing or tempted away by grandiose ideas and human plans. Jesus wants a church who continues to love him — a faithful church. This faithfulness will be seen in our relationships and the way that we love those who are outside the church and it will bear fruit as God sees a people he can trust with an open door.

The church in Philadelphia was faithful in at least two ways. It patiently endured persecution (Rev 3:10) and kept his word:

I know that you have little strength, yet you have kept my word and not denied my name.

Revelation 3:8

These Christians had hung on to the word of God and because of this had an anchor in the storm, a solid foundation, something secure to hold on to.

Faithfulness is a continuous expression of faith and faith comes by hearing the word (Romans 10:17). If we want to be faithful, we need the security of a strong faith. If we want a strong faith, we need the word of God. If we are lacking in faith and consequently lacking in faithfulness, it is probably because the word of God is not alive in our hearts. We need to hear and receive the word for faith to come forward.

We are in the midst of enormous social changes, and those changes hit high speed in the wake of the COVID-19 pandemic in early 2020. These changes could produce a time of great insecurity and uncertainty in our lives. However, social upheaval has often been a prelude to divine blessing, an outpouring of the Holy Spirit and spiritual revival--but only when God has a faithful people, established in the word, ready to take the gospel into the midst of the turmoil.

The revivals that took place across the English-speaking world in the eighteenth century occurred amidst industrial revolution, social degradation, urban unrest, and international tension. This was a period when huge numbers of inner-city populations were trapped in the addictions of gin, when technological advances like James Watts' steam engine were turning the world upside down. It was the period that included the French Revolution, Boston Tea Party and the Declaration of Independence.

Into this situation stepped a remarkable group of leaders — men like Whitefield, Wesley, Harris, Edwards and Tennant. They lived and worked in a world with huge problems and needs. The inner-city populations in England were becoming more and more prey to the distractions of the day — things which required the torture of animals, the debasement of people, and the consumption of large quantities of alcohol in the gin mills. Everywhere in Britain and America, church attendance was down and spiritual compromise and complacency were rife. Yet in the midst of this upheaval, these remarkable leaders seized the day and proclaimed the word. Their strategy of preaching in the fields, educating the poor, and training and utilizing the unordained was completely revolutionary and scandalized the church of their day. They were spiritual pioneers following the tracks left by men like Luther, Calvin and Cranmer, the pioneers of the previous generations.

The problems of our current age are similar to those in the eighteenth century. They should drive us to our knees to ask God for a fresh word and revitalized faith. If we are to emulate these Christians from Philadelphia and become like them in their life and faith, we need to model ourselves on their diet, exercise and lifestyle.

Diet — we need to take the Bible and read, mark, learn and inwardly digest it, as the old English prayer puts it, so that we can hold on to its truth in times of crisis and trust in its wisdom for the decisions we need to take.

Exercise — we must allow the difficult times to be opportunities to develop spiritual stamina and disciplines of prayer, Scripture reading, corporate worship, and witness, that hold us to our course.

Lifestyle — we need to be in the world as agents in the Kingdom but not of the world so that people will see the difference between our life with Christ and theirs without him.

Prescription — find simple repeatable ways of reading the Bible, using Scripture reading notes or a Bible reading plan. Concentrate on the basics of the Christian life —prayer, Scripture reading, fellowship with other believers and witness and ensure that they are securely part of your disciplined lifestyle. Regularly examine yourself to see whether you have taken on the attitudes of those around you or whether you are witness to something better and different.

OPEN DOORS

As we pray and build our lives on the Word, God will open the doors, sometimes in the most surprising way. A few years ago I was a minister in a small church in Brixton. Hill, London. We wanted to know where the opportunities lay in the community for witness and evangelism. We wanted to find God's open door. We decided to take a questionnaire around the community which would help us to some basic demographics — facts and figures about the community but also tell us where the opportunities lay. The key question on the survey was, 'What are the three best things about this community and what are the three worst?'

After collecting the surveys we were staggered by the results. About 95% of the people in the community saw litter on the streets to be the number one problem. At the time, Brixton Hill had one of the highest levels of infant mortality in the United Kingdom, and high incidents of family violence, street violence, and theft. So we were surprised to see that the number one problem in the area as seen by the community was something apparently so insignificant as litter. We decided to pray, and as we prayed we were reminded of the Scriptures that speak of the kingdom bringing new life and new hope.

It was as though God was showing us that the people of Brixton Hill felt as though they were the garbage of the world and that the litter on the streets represented that to them. Because it was never cleaned up, this proved to them that life was hopeless. The litter was an image of their own lives.

So we decided to have a praise march with a difference. Graham Kendrick, who lived just a few miles down the road, had begun to pioneer the March for Jesus. We took this idea and adapted it. At the time there were about sixty adults and children in the church. We got everyone together, laid out a parade route, and made a pretty rough recording of some of our favorite worship songs. Then we set out, playing the worship songs through a tape recorder strapped on to a child's pushchair and cleaning the streets as we walked and sang. The effect was amazing. Some people looked on in stunned silence. Others brought us cups of tea, juice and biscuits. One person came outside weeping as he watched what we were doing. "No one's ever done this for us before," he said. If conversations continued and if people asked us any reason for what we were doing, we told them that we wanted to show them God's love and act out a parable of what he could do in everyone's life. Praise and litter marches became a regular feature of church life. Dozens of people came into the Kingdom because of these marches. God showed us the open door, and we found a frontier ready to be won.

When Jesus sent out the 72 disciples in Luke 10, he sent them out to look for open doors. He described this as looking for a Person of Peace. This person will welcome you, feed you, care for you, and want to spend time with you. Jesus told his disciples that when they found a person of peace, they should stay with them, because that's where the open door is. You could also call a person of peace a doorkeeper or a gatekeeper.

The Christians in Philadelphia were looking for the frontier, and Jesus had opened the door. All around them were signs of chaos and collapse. It was a time of great insecurity, not only for them but for everyone else in the world. To these Christians who were holding on, God gave the comforting words that they would not only have an open door in the present, but also a home with him forever. To these people who had been excluded from the synagogue, God said he would make them fixtures inside his temple. To these Christians who had to deal with marginalization and change, God said they would never leave his presence. In the past they had to live with being nobodies with uncertain futures. But now he says, "I'll give you my name and address and I will use permanent ink to write with" From heaven's perspective our identity and our home is tied up with God. We have his name and his address written all over us.

> *Him who overcomes I will make a pillar in the temple of my God. Never again will he leave it. I will write on him the name of my God and the name of the city of my God, the new Jerusalem, which is coming down out of heaven from my God; and I will also write on him my new name*'

Revelation 3:12

CRISIS AND CULTURAL EARTHQUAKES: THE CONNECTING STORY

The church at Philadelphia faced a crisis of excommunication. How difficult it must have been for them to even have their religious institutions shaken! While excommunication in our day may be rarer, this phenomenon still happens. It happened when worship services and church choirs and other groups became places where the coronavirus infected dozens. It happened when churches couldn't meet together for months on end because of state of emergency declarations. It also happens when pastors fall because of financial crimes or abuse allegations. We have all seen even our churches shaken.

Our confidence and clarity cannot come from our churches. Instead, we need to look at the connecting story of God.

> *Keep your lives free from the love of money and be*
> *content with what you have, God has said,*
> > *"Never will I leave you;*
> > *never will I forsake you."*
>
> *So we say with confidence,*
> > *"The Lord is my helper; I will not be afraid*
> > *What can mere mortals do to me?"*
>
> *Remember your leaders, who spoke the word of God*
> *to you. Consider the outcome of their way of life and*
> *imitate their faith. Jesus Christ is the same yesterday and*
> *today and forever.*

Hebrews 13:5-6

Our connecting story leads us to our leaders, who were also part of the story of God. They have revealed the connecting story to us. This story connects us to Scripture itself, because we are children and representatives of the same God that they were. That same God reveals grace and mercy to kindness to us, and Scripture reveals this to us.

Looking to the connecting story gives us a broader perspective of the shaking in our time. It gives us greater cultural intelligence. And it gives us clarity that allows our hearts to be secure. Jesus is the same yesterday, today, and forever. He is our compass, and by following him we find a connecting story that cannot be shaken. So we can orient our lives around Jesus instead of around ourselves, and then live with clarity and courage and compassion and community.

HUDDLE STUDY GUIDE

Why did God allow the excommunication in Philadelphia? What larger narrative, what connecting story, was in play?

What open doors are before you? How can you move through these open doors? How can our Huddle and our church do this together?

Why are pioneers important? Why are settlers important? What does it look like when they work together well? What does it look like when they don't?

FOR ADDITIONAL REFLECTION

Pioneers and Settlers

Are you more of a pioneer or a settler? This personal assessment will help you discover this part of your identity. Consider each of these statements. If you agree strongly give yourself 10, if you disagree give yourself 1.

1. I enjoy change and do not see it as a threat.
2. I appreciate careful preparation before action.
3. I like to ensure that others will come along with me in new endeavours.
4. Being adaptable is my strength.
5. I try to bring everyone along with me even if this means moving more slowly.
6. I become bored easily if I do the same thing for too long.
7. I like to have an idea of the outcome before I start a project.
8. I find it difficult when others do not immediately respond to fresh insights.
9. I believe that careful planning avoids unnecessary hurt and upset.
10. I like to think through the details before I act.
11. I enjoy the challenge of a new situation.
12. I become impatient with a slow decision-making process.

If you add the scores for questions 1, 4, 6, 8, 11, 12 you get your 'pioneering' score. Write it down below.

If you add the scores for questions 2, 3, 5, 7, 9, 10 you get your 'settler' score. Write it down below.

We all have some of both 'pioneer' and 'settler' in us. The two scores shows whether you have more of one than the other.

PIONEER SCORE:

SETTLER SCORE:

Reflect on what you find here, and then discuss it with your Huddle or another group to determine what God is telling you and what you should do about it. One follow-up question to consider: How well are you doing at working together with someone who is the opposite of you? Where might God be leading you to change?

7

LAODECIA
A CRISIS OF LUKEWARMNESS

To the angel of the church in Laodicea write:

These are the words of the Amen, the faithful and true witness, the ruler of God's creation. I know your deeds, that you are neither cold nor hot. I wish you were either one or the other! So, because you are lukewarm—neither hot nor cold—I am about to spit you out of my mouth. You say, 'I am rich; I have acquired wealth and do not need a thing.' But you do not realize that you are wretched, pitiful, poor, blind and naked. I counsel you to buy from me gold refined in the fire, so you can become rich; and white clothes to wear, so you can cover your shameful nakedness; and salve to put on your eyes, so you can see.

Those whom I love I rebuke and discipline. So be earnest and repent. Here I am! I stand at the door and knock. If anyone hears my voice and opens the door, I will come in and eat with that person, and they with me.

To the one who is victorious, I will give the right to sit

with me on my throne, just as I was victorious and sat
down with my Father on his throne. Whoever has ears,
let them hear what the Spirit says to the churches.

Revelation 3:14-22

During the early 1990s, my family and I lived in the USA.
We did a number of exciting and challenging things. One was
spending some time on the staff of Trinity Cathedral in Little
Rock, Arkansas. The Cathedral is situated within the inner urban
area and the oldest part of Little Rock. Traveling back and forth
daily to work at the Cathedral from my home in the suburbs gave
me a fresh perspective on what has become a familiar problem.

Within walking distance of my office in Trinity Cathedral, all
of life met. To the north lay the new freeway which divided
the commercial and residential districts of downtown Little
Rock. On the residential side lay two disused church buildings,
one of which — the one I could see from my office window
— had been converted into apartments which were rented to
young professionals who had recently left college to begin their
new careers. The other church building was up for sale. Its
congregation had moved to the more pleasant surroundings of
the west Little Rock suburbs. To the east, little more than a block
away, a burned out crack house was found among the bars, cafés
and small, often struggling businesses of Main Street. One block
to the south, amid fine Victorian homes, lay the Governor's
mansion, former home of Bill, Hillary and Chelsea Clinton. A
block west and you came to Broadway, the well-known black
college, Philander Smith, and one of the poorest communities in
the city.

During the year that I was working at the Cathedral, the
community visibly deteriorated. The crack house was not
refurbished. More groups of what appeared to be aimless youths

gathered in the streets, and the crime statistics for the area and the city as a whole escalated apparently out of control. I have since returned on a number of occasions, and the reports are just as bad, if not worse.

Enormous problems and huge potential are locked in mortal combat on the streets of downtown Little Rock, and it looks as if the problems are gaining the upper hand. What was once a melting pot is now a sinkhole. Poverty is growing. Drug and alcohol abuse is at epidemic levels. Gang warfare and violent crime are so common that they are hardly newsworthy. Stable families are a thing of the past. Whole neighborhoods are degenerating into barbarism. The cauldron of the inner city has boiled over in conflict.

We are seeing these riots and vandalism on the streets today in increasing numbers. Many cities in USA are facing looting and crime at unprecedented levels. The fault lines in our country are growing daily.

RETREATING FROM PROBLEMS

Across the western world, the tide of spiritual and social sickness continues to rise. The most common response within the church is shock, bewilderment, and corporate retreat. The churches in the northern hemisphere, and particularly those in America, have followed the money and moved to the suburbs. The largest, strongest, and most prosperous churches are almost always found there. Where this is not the case, and large churches continue to worship in facilities found within the inner city or commercial centers, the congregations are largely drawn from the suburbs or wealthy areas of the city.

Having worked both as a leader in an inner-city church and a suburban church, it is quite clear to me that western Christianity has a tendency to disengage from the poor and move away from areas of need. There are, of course, always notable exceptions, but numerically and financially the church's strength is found among the wealthy. Wealth tends to isolate us from the problems of the world and insulate us from the needs of others. It also clouds our judgement. It is amazing how often you hear wealthy Christians blame the poor for their own problems. Perhaps the best we can expect from wealthy Christians is a lukewarm response to need, because the reality which confronts them is so unfamiliar and alien. It is difficult to make an adequate response to a situation from which you are detached. It is difficult to motivate yourself to act on behalf of others if you have already blamed them for the problems they face. If left unchecked, this is a course that will lead only to disaster.

When the church has responded to the needs of the poor with blame and inaction, the society of which it is part has been put into a perilous position. During the 18th century, the social disturbances in France resulted in the French Revolution and a social tragedy of vast proportions. The same social upheavals led to revival in Britain under Whitefield and Wesley. The difference between two nations was found in the response of those who called themselves Christians. In France, the church remained aloof and unconcerned about the needs of the poor, and although this was true of the majority of the church in Britain, some of the pioneering leaders took the gospel to the streets, and society was transformed.

Wealth and power tend to cloud our judgement and cause us to minimize the problems that we face. A familiar story may serve to illustrate. On April 14, 1912, the sea was calm as the Titanic cut through the chilly waters of the North Atlantic. The calm conditions allowed a fog to settle, and although visibility was becoming poor, the Titanic's engine rooms were running at full steam. Icebergs had been reported by other ships in the area, but still the Titanic forged ahead. A watch was set in the crow's nest and on the bridge. The unsinkable ship continued to cruise at full speed hoping to reach New York ahead of time.

The man in the crow's nest barely had time to call the bridge before the Titanic struck the iceberg. His hurried message was received, and the bridge signaled a turn to starboard at the last moment so that the liner struck a glancing blow which showered shards of ice all along the decks of the ocean liner. At first there seemed nothing to worry about, but the cavalier attitude of captain and crew soon began to erode as the ship started to list and take on water.

News came from the engine rooms that a number of the watertight compartments were flooded, including the engine room. At first this did not seem to present a danger to life. Captain Smith and his crew knew that the ship would stay afloat even if four of the compartments were flooded. This perhaps explains their somewhat half-hearted response to the situation. Unfortunately, five of the compartments were flooded, and the ship quickly sank claiming the lives of more than 1,500 people. The unthinkable had happened. An unsinkable ship had sunk!

Many of those who lost their lives made no attempt to escape as the ship went down. Reports persist of the orchestra playing in the ballroom even as the ship was sinking. A great number of those who wanted to escape could not find refuge in a lifeboat. The ship had provided enough boats for little more than half the passengers. Others who had tried to escape perished after less than ten minutes in the icy waters.

The only other ship in the area, the Californian, did not hear the distress signals from the Titanic — its wireless room was unmanned that night. As hundreds of survivors struggled to stay alive on the open waters, the Californian continued her course less than twenty miles from the scene. The survivors had to wait an hour and twenty minutes for the Cunard liner the Carpathia to find them. Her captain, Arthur Henry Rostron, acted promptly on hearing news of the Titanic's predicament and steamed at full speed to the scene of the disaster, making preparations for the survivors as they went. On arrival the Carpathia crisscrossed the area looking for and picking up survivors.

When the first light came, the passengers and crew saw a remarkable sight. The ocean was littered with icebergs both large and small. It was amazing that the Titanic had not come to grief earlier in its reckless journey across the North Atlantic, and just as remarkable that the Carpathia had not suffered a similar fate as it sailed full steam through the night to the scene of the disaster.

The sinking was completely unexpected, and so little or no preparation was made for such an event. Caution should have marked the actions of the owners, the captain and crew. Only the quick thinking and sacrificial action of Captain Rostron and the Carpathia prevented further tragedy.

The owners and passengers of the Titanic were mostly wealthy people. They assumed that their wealth had brought them the certainty of an unsinkable ship, but unfortunately this same wealth and power had only led them to believe a lie and to act foolishly in a dangerous environment. The half-hearted, lukewarm response of the captain and crew was an example of the same malaise and denial of reality found among the passengers as they greeted the news that the ship was going down.

I hope the church during its present crisis is not going to be rearranging the deck chairs aboard the titanic as it sinks. Now is the time we need to look hard into the face of the crisis and what we are responsible for through our own ignorance, privilege and laziness.

MAKING IT PERSONAL

We have looked at the big picture of how wealth can alienate us from contemporary social problems, and we have seen a historical example of how wealth and power gave an unrealistic sense of security. But this is also true of the small picture in our own lives. If our material needs are met, we begin to assume that we are spiritually healthy as well. This can lead us into a false sense of security and an unhelpful and unbiblical view of our fundamental needs.

The church in Laodicea was in just such a crisis. Its wealth and power had led it to miss the spiritual realities of its situation. The text of the letter speaks eloquently of an impending tragedy: "These are the words of the Amen."

All the other letters use pictures drawn from the vision of Jesus in chapter 1. This is the only letter among the seven in which Jesus uses a description of himself which is not drawn from this vision. Perhaps he wanted to shake the church out of its sloth and self-satisfaction, or perhaps the Lord wanted simply to remind them that he and not they had the last word — he was the Amen.

The other words of Jesus in this letter connected to life in Laodicea, to help the Christians there make his words personal.

I am the faithful and true witness, the rules of God's creation.

Laodicea was a city well known among the legal profession as the city where the regional courthouse could be found. Jesus is saying, "I am the faithful and true witness, and I have a case against you. My charge is that you are lukewarm. My evidence is that you are neither hot nor cold."

Laodicea was in the dock. They were guilty as charged. In addressing the church in this way, Jesus follows a familiar pattern of using situations and experiences that the Christians would recognize and understand to describe their spiritual state. The Court of Assize was held here. Now Jesus was standing as a witness against them.

I know your deeds, that you are neither cold nor hot.

The water in the town came from hot springs across the valley, arriving in Laodicea lukewarm via aqueducts. The Christians were neither hot nor cold.

Because you are lukewarm — neither hot nor cold — I am about to spit you out of my mouth.

Laodicea was in a desperate state. Jesus was thoroughly sick of these Christians. They were neither one thing nor another, and so they were about to find out how seriously he took this situation

You say, "I am rich; I have acquired wealth and do not need a thing.'

Like Sardis, Laodicea was well-known for its wealth and power. As well as being a legal center, it was a center for trade and banking. It was so wealthy that when it was destroyed in AD 17 by an earthquake that affected many of the other cities in the region, it was rebuilt entirely at its own expense. Even Sardis had to borrow money from Rome to rebuild, but not Laodicea. Laodicea was rich and it was proud of the fact.

But you do not realize that you are wretched, pitiful, poor, blind and naked.

As a trading center, Laodicea was known for its clothing trade. The black woollen garments that the sheep of the region produced were highly prized, and the Phrygian eye salve, known throughout the world as a remedy for sore eyes, was made and sold here. As in Sardis, the Laodicean church seems to have picked up the spirit of the community around them. Instead of being different from the world, these Christians had become dominated by worldly attitudes. Like others in the city the Christians felt that they had achieved much and were well respected, holding a place of honor among the cities of the region.

Jesus wanted to remind them that everything good that they had received was a gift from him. Because they saw themselves as the source of their wealth and well-being, these material gifts were meaningless. They were actually pitiful, wretched, and poor. Even though they were clothed in rich and fashionable garments, they were vulnerable in their self-centeredness, and were spiritually naked. Though they had the best remedy available at the time for sore eyes and failing sight, they were blind to the reality of their situation. Their half-hearted spirituality had left them thinking that they were rich and not in need of anything, but Jesus reminded them that they were living without the grace of his presence and the gifts that he bestows.

How could they have gotten themselves into such a terrible state? What was the solution and where might we learn from their crisis of lukewarmness?

LUKEWARM LIVES

When I have a bath, I like to get it as hot as possible, just about to the point where it peels off my skin. Having got in I very quickly become aware that the water is cooling down. Sometimes I will add water from the hot tap. At other times I just lie back and read a book and soak in the hot water. As the water cools, I often find myself trying to get more submerged until it appears that only my face and hands are exposed. At this point the most difficult thing to do is to get out and confront the cold air.

The Christians in Laodicea had started out in the heat of spiritual revival. The church was planted in a period of great blessing and spiritual outpouring. Instead of returning to the source of that spiritual warmth and seeking regular renewal and refreshment, the Laodiceans had somehow become immersed in their own lives and culture. They did not realize that the warmth of God's presence was receding and the temperature of their spiritual lives was growing colder by the minute.

The water that came from the hot springs in Hierapolis reached the city lukewarm, milky white, and clouded with the deposits from the limestone rocks. The people of Laodicea often found that the water caused sickness and vomiting if they did not either allow it to cool or boil it first. Cold water was useful and refreshing. Hot water could be used for all kinds of things. But tepid water was so distasteful that all you could do was spit it out.

Jesus said to the Christians in Laodicea, "You are lukewarm. You turn my stomach. You make me sick. All I want to do is spit you out." Such a statement surely got their attention! But what were they to do?

"I counsel you to buy from me gold refined in the fire, so that you can become rich; and white clothes to wear, so that you can cover your shameful nakedness; and salve to put on your eyes, so that you can see."

The first thing they needed was to receive the fresh insight that Jesus was offering. They needed to recognize their desperate need for him and the dire straits that they were in. Once this revelation had broken through, Jesus knew that they would cry out in their need. To this need he offers the pure, refined gold of his presence — the white clothes of his holiness and the healing salve of his word that .would help them to see themselves as he saw them — as poor people made rich, as naked people reclothed, as blind people able to see, as needy people with their needs met.

A COMMON PROBLEM

The problems of Laodicea are common to us all. We all belong to a generation which is perhaps the richest the world has ever seen. From the perspective of the poorest people in the world, we are very well off. Although we may not be rich in comparison with the richest, in comparison with the poorest we certainly are.

Riches lead us into a trap. We become secure in them and dependent upon them to provide us with everything we need. We assume that everything has come from our own hands.

But there is a fundamental corrective to this point of view: Neither we nor our wealth can rescue us from our fundamental predicament. We cannot know God unless he reveals himself. We cannot be free from guilt unless he forgives us. We are unable to know life in all its fullness unless he makes it known to us. The Bible tells us that we are rescued only by his goodness, by his grace. The truth is that, far from being rich, we are in debt; if you know God, you are in debt; if you have been filled with the Spirit, you are in debt; if God answers your prayer, you are in debt! The truth is we have nothing which we can call our own that is not a gift from him. And so if we have more than others, we should be even more grateful.

At the beginning of the chapter; I spoke about the response of the wealthy suburban churches to the needs of the poor. When we recognize that all we have, even if we "earned" it, is a gift from God, we tend to become less critical of others and more conscious of our responsibility.

My personal experience is that my readiness to criticize or ignore the plight of others is usually in direct relation to how lukewarm I have become in my response to God. It is the "hot" Christian who goes to the mission field. It is the committed Christian who is prepared to sacrifice from the riches of their life that others may live. Wealth quickly leads to lukewarmness, and lukewarmness always leads to a lessening of commitment and diminishing of our witness.

Being grateful means that we give God the recognition that is his due and we move away from the self-reliance and self-centeredness into which we so easily fall. We move back to the source that can heat us again and deliver us from our lukewarmness. We recognize our debt and also that the debt is paid and we give God the glory that a situation that we were unable to solve he has stepped into and changed for good.

Those whom I love I rebuke, and discipline. So be earnest, and repent. Here I am! I stand at the door and knock. If anyone hears my voice and opens the door, I will come in and eat with him, and he with me.

In this chapter I have spoken quite deliberately and directly about the dangers of wealth. The reasons for this are that I see them as very real dangers in my own life and challenges for the church

which I now lead. Several decades ago, my work was almost
exclusively given over to the poorest and most alienated in society.
My wife and I raised our children in the inner city. Since then, I
have led churches in much more affluent areas. I know too well
how easy it is to become distanced from many of the realities
that the majority of people face and what a simple step it would
be for us as a church to become self-satisfied in our spiritual and
material success.

The truth is that our fundamental problems are the same as
everyone else's. Our basic needs are no different from anyone
else's, and the solution is the same — Jesus. I know that I must
not allow myself to drift into the unprotected place of spiritual
pride and materialistic self-centredness. That would be like sailing
a ship at full speed in an ocean full of icebergs. I need to hear the
corrective of God's word and submit to his rebuke, knowing that
it only arises from his heart of love.

KNOCKING AT THE DOOR

But what is it like to hear this rebuke and invite Jesus to change
our hearts? It is like hearing him knock at a door and opening it
to let him in. Opening the door requires our conscious, deliberate
effort, but keeping it open also requires some effort. While we
await the return of Christ, sin is still a factor to be reckoned with.
It is as though the door of our hearts has a return spring. When
we do not consciously welcome him into the moments of our day,
we almost immediately begin to exclude him. The return spring
begins to tug, and the door slowly closes. This does not mean
that Jesus abandons us or that we lose our position as the adopted
children of God. It simply means that we begin to miss out on
the blessing that his consciously recognized presence brings to
each situation.

One of the classic works on prayer is a book by the Norwegian teacher and pastor Ole Hallesby. In it he teaches that one of the keys to effective prayer is to recognize that it is always initiated by God himself. Reflecting on Revelation 3.20, he says, "To pray is to let Jesus come into our hearts" (Hallesby, *Prayer*, Augsburg, Book 1, p 11).

Prayer is much more opening the door of our lives to him as he knocks than knocking at the door of heaven and hoping that he will open the door to us. Every time we remember to pray, every time we speak to him, it is because we have heard his voice and recognized his knock at the door. Remembering this our prayers will usually begin with gratitude at his initiative and be free from the self-centred striving that often accompanies them.

As a pastor I have often been aware of the guilt that so often accompanies the prayer life of ordinary Christians. I have often been told how guilty someone feels because they are not praying. Unfortunately, guilt is not a great motivator toward action. But gratitude is.

When we realize that God is constantly reaching out to us, speaking to us, drawing us, and calling our name, prayer becomes more of a response than an initiative. We may feel guilty at times that we do not listen, but knowing that God never stops calling brings great freedom. He continues to speak to us, continues to draw us even when we do not respond. His commitment to us is constant and faithful and our part within prayer is simply to respond.

Try it next time you pray! Remember that you are responding to his prompting, and not trying to get his attention. See whether it begins to change some of your attitudes toward your prayer life.

BIRTHRIGHT

One other thing to remember as you pray: It is your birthright as a Christian to hear the voice of Jesus. It's not a special gift given to some people. It's not a task that is provided to preachers and the pastors. It is the birthright of every Christian.

In John 10, when Jesus describes the relationship between himself as the Good Shepherd and those who follow him, his sheep, says, "My sheep hear my voice." It's not that they could if they really tried hard. It's not if they pray and read their Bibles every day, It's that they do.

So what's the qualification for hearing the voice of Jesus? Knowing him. That's it. The qualification is simply that you are a sheep following the shepherd. Now you might say that you don't feel like you're very good at it. Actually, that's a good place to start.

The truth that hearing God's voice is the birthright of every Christian is the definitive statement of the gospel. Why is it definitive? Because it's the very first gospel presentation of the newborn church on the day of Pentecost. You can't get more definitive than that. Peter preaches the definitive proclamation of the gospel, and when he's preaching that definitive proclamation of the gospel and answering the questions that are in the hearts and minds of his hearers, he says that what you see here and what you're witness to today is what was prophesied in the past.

This birthright is what God has given you as his greatest gift. And it doesn't matter how young you are or how old you are or how familiar you are with hearing the voice of Jesus.

Some will say that you think you hear the voice of Jesus when reading the Bible. That's great! But remember that most of the people Jesus addresses in this letter did not have a Bible. The canon of scripture was not closed until the middle of the third century. Nobody could carry a Bible around in the first-century church. Picture a wheelbarrow full of scrolls, and it's easy to see why. Books weren't invented yet! If you went to the synagogue, you would find some scrolls of the Old Testament, but nobody carried them around.

So what did people do? They memorized Scripture. And when you memorize Scripture, you are able to test what you think you hear against what Scripture says. This allows you to clearly determine what Jesus is saying. The written word is intended to give you access to the living word who speaks to you daily, who speaks to you hourly, who speaks to you moment by moment.

Scripture reveals some of the ways God communicates through stories from the church's early life. Take Revelation 1 for example. When John is first attending to this amazing vision of the glorified Jesus ascended and risen, every part of him is engaged in listening to what the risen Lord Jesus communicates. Jesus speaks, and it's like a trumpet. He reveals himself, and it's a vision that is of cinematic quality. John is so overwhelmed by what he sees that his body reacts and he falls down. And when he is prostrated on the floor, the very voice of Jesus extends to him as the hand of Jesus is placed on his right shoulder.

So don't restrict the way in which God is going to speak to you. He may speak to you as you watch the sunrise, as you watch the children play, or as you listen to the birds singing in the trees. It may be that God will communicate to you with the kindness of a person's touch or the graciousness of a person's smile. As we learn to attend to the voice of Jesus, still more, and as we test what we hear against the written word, so we will become more and more familiar with walking with Jesus daily. I know people will think you're crazy. That's OK. I know your friends will think you're mad. That's fine. This is our calling, our birthright, and our heritage.

DINING WITH JESUS

When we open the door to Jesus and listen to him, he comes and shares our experience. He eats with us, and the wonderful thing is that he brings food with him to share, and in what he offers he gives us a foretaste of heaven. As we continue to commune with him in this way, the certainty of heaven grows in our hearts. We recognize that God is waiting to welcome us, not only into his presence, but on to his throne.

To him who overcomes, I will give the right to sit with me on my throne, just as I overcame and sat down with my Father on his throne

When our children were growing up, we tried to eat dinner together every evening. Most weekdays after our evening meal, I disappeared to the lounge to watch the Six O'Clock News. The children often giggled and made fun of the fact that they knew exactly what I was going to say. I began the sentence, "I'm just going to..." and all three chimed in, "'watch the news!" Partly they were giggling because I said it every night, and partly because I fell asleep watching it.

Watching the news became a special time of quiet for me when I reclined in my favorite chair and for thirty minutes found my own space. The kids were right of course. Often I fell asleep. Every so often one of them snuck into the lounge and snuggled down beside me and quietly whispered, "Is it all right if I watch with you for a little while?" As a father I found this request almost impossible to refuse, because what my children were saying is that they wanted to share not only my chair and my time, but also my quiet.

With God we do not even have to ask if we can share these things. He says, "I have made room for my Son on my throne, Now I am making room for you too. Come and rest under the protection of my arm. Come and climb up into my lap." The place reserved for us is the place of greatest intimacy because it is the place where God freely invites us to share his experience of authority and rest.

Jesus has sat down with the Father, and together with the Holy Spirit they are making room for us now that we might sit with them forever. We will know the intimacy of their presence constantly sharing with each member of the Trinity (Father, Son and, Holy Spirit) the responsibility of ruling and reigning in the new creation.

CRISIS AND CULTURAL EARTHQUAKES: ESCAPING LUKEWARMNESS

It's hard to be lukewarm during times of crisis. But as the crisis ebbs, we may be tempted to return to our typical way of life. This doesn't just mean things like going to restaurants, as so many people were eager to do after the COVID-19 quarantine. It also means settling back into a routine and the lukewarmness toward God that we were in before crisis struck.

As we conclude our consideration of crisis, it's important to think about what happens afterward. We need to learn the lessons of crisis that can lead to personal revival.

I remember hearing Martin Lloyd-Jones preach a sermon around the story from the Old Testament where Isaac once again dug the wells of his father Abraham (Gen. 26:18). It's a great picture of what we can do. In times of personal retreat--going back to familiar ground, and excavating the life-giving water Jesus gives us. As we do this, we re-engage with our God-given identity and with the connecting story we find in Scripture about Jesus who is the same yesterday, today, and forever. As we do, the word of God strengthens us and gives us a sword in our hands against enemy temptations.

So we need times of retreat. And as we spend time with God, we will experience the kind of shaking not of crisis but of the Spirit of God. Like the disciples in the upper room before Pentecost, God will shake us out of lukewarmness to live in power so that we can bring his Kingdom and lead others to the connecting story of Jesus who saves today just as he did yesterday and just as he will do tomorrow.

HUDDLE STUDY GUIDE

Reflect on the truth that Jesus knocks at the door of our lives. What does this tell us about Jesus? What does it tell us about our connecting with Jesus?

What happens when we open the door to Jesus? How do we do this?

How can we walk with Jesus every day? How can we encourage each other to do this?

8

THE HEART
OF THE MATTER

These are the words of him...

who holds the seven stars in his right hand and walks among the seven golden lampstands ...

who is the First and the Last, who died and came to life again ...

who has the sharp double-edged sword ...

whose eyes are like blazing fire and whose feet are like burnished bronze ...

who holds the seven spirits of God and the seven stars

who is holy and true, who holds the key of David of the Amen, the faithful and true witness, the ruler of God's Creation.

(Combined from all seven letters)

We know from our own lives that our health and our hearts are closely connected. When the Bible speaks of hearts, it usually means the center of our being, the place from which our thought and emotion, attitudes and motivations, flow. Jesus said: "Out of the overflow of his heart his mouth speaks" (Luke 6:45).

If we have good things stored up in our hearts, good things will flow from our lives. If we have bad things in our hearts, we can only expect bad things to be produced by them. Physically, if our hearts are healthy we have a much better chance of the rest of our bodies being healthy. The same is true of our relationship with God. The things that Jesus says to his churches strike to the very heart of their needs and where necessary deal with the spiritual maladies that are growing up within them.

All of the letters begin with the risen Lord Jesus revealing something about himself. To each situation that the church confronts, Jesus is the answer. For every problem that we face, he is the solution.

To Ephesus, the leading church among the seven, he says that it was he who held the messengers of his word — the stars, it was he who oversaw churches as he walked among the lampstands. Perhaps their responsibilities had caused them to become overburdened and unfocused, thus losing their first love. He reminded them that he is the center of the picture — the church is his responsibility and they needed to relate to him. When they looked to him his love would flow to them, and their love for him and others would be released.

To Smyrna, the small church struggling to hold on in the face of persecution, Jesus was the First and the Last. They had nothing to fear about the future because he sees the end from the beginning. He oversaw their whole life from its start to its conclusion, and as they faced the prospect of death, he reminded them that he has overcome death. Because they knew him, they will do so as well.

To Pergamum, unable to discern the difference between truth and error, he came with his word which is sharp and double-edged. He is the truth personified, and so when he is at the center, at the heart of our lives, he is able to divide right from wrong. Pergamum was a church that had not learned enough of the truth of God's Word to protect them from error. When Jesus came wielding his sword, the truth would set them free.

To Thyatira, where the church had become so permissive that it allowed teaching that led to immorality, he came with fire. The fire that poured from his blazing eyes and burning feet and would consume the dross and purify the church. Jesus disciplines those whom he loves. When he comes to consume the sin in our life, he does so because his love will not allow us to continue in the desperate state that sin produces.

To the church in Sardis, which was almost dead, he came with the offer of life. It is he who dispatches the sevenfold spirit of God. It is he who releases the messengers of God's word to bring life. To receive this life, these Christians would need to open the eyes that had become closed with sleep. They would need to awaken out of their complacency and inactivity to receive the offer of his energizing life-giving Spirit.

To the church that had been locked out of the synagogue, Philadelphia, he told them that he holds the key to every door, one of which he opened for them. He reminded them that he is in charge, and that although the devil may have had plans to harm them, he only had plans to bless them. As the devil shuts one door, Jesus opens another. As one opportunity for life and witness seems to be removed, Jesus ensures that fresh opportunities are waiting for us.

To Laodicea, a church taken up with its own status and wealth, he said that he was the ruler. He is in charge and a solution to their unfaithfulness, He also offered himself as the faithful and true witness. Even though these Christians were lukewarm about their faith (a lukewarmness that made Jesus sick), in his love he continued to take the initiative with these wayward Christians. He came knocking at the door of their hearts, seeking to gain entrance that he might bless and heal them.

THE SPIRITUAL HEALTH OF OUR HEARTS

When it comes to our spiritual health, Jesus is the heart of the matter. When it comes to our response to what he offers, our spiritual health becomes a matter of the heart. The wonder of Jesus is that he is able to meet us where we are and take us to where we need to be. Whatever circumstance, he meets us as Lord. Whatever sin, he comes to us as Savior.

Our spiritual health finally depends on him. Our spiritual well-being is tied up in our relationship with the living Lord Jesus. When he spoke to the hearts of these early Christians, his words rang out for eternity. As we listen today the effect is the same.

When Jesus addressed the needs of these seven churches, he spoke to people with different levels of spiritual health. It was as though he was revealing different kinds of hearts that reflected different levels of spiritual health. Some of the Christians had healthy hearts, but some had developed hard hearts. Still others were in danger of becoming faint or half-hearted.

When we examine ourselves in the light of God's Word, our hearts are exposed and laid bare. However reluctant we might be to the work of God's cleansing and empowering within us, eventually we will have to ask, "What kind of heart do I have and what kind of heart do I want?"

If our hearts are healthy, surely everything else will follow suit. Ephesus had forsaken its first love and had begun to develop a hard heart. Love keeps our hearts soft. Sharing love keeps our hearts warm. When we move away from our first love, our hearts begin to grow cold and hard. Harshness marks our words, and a critical spirit supplants generosity and kindness.

Our hearts — our spiritual core — also become hard when we move away from our source of life. When a heart begins to die, it becomes inflexible. Sardis was in this state. They had exchanged the things that led to life for the pursuit of things that led to death, and their heart was suffering as a consequence.

Hard and cold hearts become anxious and full of worry. Soft hearts, full of life and love, know the security and peace of God's presence. Our society is riddled with stress and fear. They stalk and hunt us down. If we try to go it alone, declaring our independence from God, saying in not so many words that we can manage on our own, our hearts will degenerate into this kind of spiritual sickness. The effects will be that our experience is marked by the same stress and fear as those around us.

The solution to a cold or a hard heart is to embrace again the fire of his love which will melt and renew our hearts and cause them to overflow with the life we once knew. It is the love that first captured our hearts that we need to return to if our hearts are to be healed. It is not a healing that we can find from anywhere else or work up from within, but only one that flows out of God's heart of love for us.

The churches in Pergamum and Thyatira were not calloused by a hardness of heart, but were compromised by faintness of heart. They feared the consequences of rejection and persecution. They produced man-made solutions to circumstances that only God could change. Their fear for themselves, and their faintheartedness in the face of spiritual battle, left them open to deception as they were offered a way out from the circumstances that threatened to overwhelm them.

For some the compromise had become so complete that they were indistinguishable from the worst examples of those who lived around them. Being indistinguishable meant that they were camouflaged within their society. Because no one knew they were there, no one objected to their presence. Because no one knew what they believed they could not be persecuted for their faith.

These churches had exchanged the battle of the Christian life for a fight with God. Jesus promised that he would not only come to war against them with his Word, but that he would win and they would know the loss of it. These Christians were afraid for their lives. They lived in the midst of persecution.

Perhaps if we were given the same options as they were, we would buckle under the pressure as well. But compromise comes in varying degrees and differing guises. There is the compromise in our conversation as we seek to be included among our peers and workmates. There is the compromise of the truth when we hear error and do not challenge it. There is the compromise of relationships where we surrender what is right because we want to be loved by those who want to do wrong.

What is the solution to a faint heart? What we need is strength, but strength that comes from ourselves is only cleverly disguised weakness. We need the strength of the Lord that is made perfect in our weakness.

Where would this strength come from? It comes from God himself as we offer him our fears, our weaknesses, our tendency toward compromise. When we face ourselves with the reality of our hearts and offer these to God in prayer, his promise is that he will strengthen us with his power and life.

Laodicea, the self-reliant church, had become half-hearted in its response to God. They wanted him and all his gifts, but they wanted the benefits of the world as well. Half of their heart they gave to him, and half they kept for themselves. They were holding on to both life and death.

Though they did not recognize it, their situation was dire. Self-centredness quickly develops into self-reliance, and the best we can expect is a half-hearted response to God and his word.

The psalmist says,"'Lord, give me an undivided heart, that I may fear your name" (Psalm 86:11). A divided heart keeps back a portion of our lives for ourselves. It may be our thoughts, fantasies, ideas of self-grandeur, or pet sins that we do not want to surrender. All this leaves us in an unhealthy state with a spiritual sickness that can only worsen. The answer is to surrender wholeheartedly to God and allow him through every door into every part of our life.

Two churches did not have hard hearts, faint hearts or a half-hearted response to God, but had soft hearts. These were Smyrna and Philadelphia. Jesus was pleased with these Christians. They held on in the midst of difficulty. They kept his word and did not waver. Because of this, though the world laughed at their weakness, they were strong in the Lord. Though they were ridiculed for their faith, they were spiritually healthy and able to receive all that God had in store for them.

In the letter to the church of Thyatira, Jesus says, "I am he who searches hearts and minds." He is able to search our motivations and intentions. He looks from the inside to the outside. He knows our hearts.

John wrote this letter from a labor camp on the Isle of Patmos. He probably thought he would die there, although historical texts indicate that he eventually returned to Ephesus and died there. But in his quarantine on Patmos, John maintained a soft heart toward Jesus. It was so soft that when Jesus came to him, John responded not only personally, but also on behalf of others by writing down this vision to become the last book of the Bible. Jesus had searched John's heart and mind and knew that John was prepared to be his messenger to these seven churches and across thousands of years to countless churches throughout history.

So what is Jesus saying about your heart? Is he calling you to a softer heart? A stronger heart? An undivided heart? How is Jesus prompting you to repent and believe so that you live wholehearted for him? Remember, who have ears should hear what Jesus is saying. Let the letters to these churches prompt you as you listen to what Jesus is saying about your heart here and now.

TRIUMPH IN THE END

In the first chapter, I told of a vision that I had in the Forest of Dean, a vision of the battle taking place in the spiritual realm over the church. The devil and his minions may well be right in their assessment of many churches as being likely to give up the fight before he does. There are always those churches who reveal a more faithful and determined attitude, churches like Smyrna and Philadelphia. But humanly speaking that would not be enough to win the fight against deception and evil that the church is called into.

Fortunately for us, the battle and the ultimate victory does not depend on us, or even on our ability to be faithful. It depends

on God's sovereignty and power to do what he chooses. One
of the great mysteries of our faith is that God chooses to work
through us and even appears to limit himself in the short term
to our ability to respond. But God will win. What he has begun,
he will finish. What he is determined to do, he will complete.
His determination is this — to beat down evil and raise up his
goodness. In doing this he will most certainly defeat the devil and
all his demons, redeeming the church and presenting her as his
beloved and chosen one. God is determined to reveal his goodness
and mercy to his church and through his church. She will be like
a beautiful bride on display for all the world to see, as he comes
and claims her for his own.

The book of Revelation begins with the letters to the churches,
but ends with the triumphal proclamation of God's certain
victory. The truth is this: Jesus is returning to claim his church
and present her as his bride, and when this happens, as it surely
will, God will reveal his new creation — a new heaven and a new
earth — prepared for his people to inhabit.

> *Behold, I am coming soon! My reward is with me, and
> I will give to everyone according to what he has done. I
> am the Alpha and the Omega, the First and the Last, the
> Beginning and the End.*

Revelation 22:12,13

What then is our task as we respond to this great work of God?
We are to cooperate with God and allow him to make us into the
bride of Christ in all her beauty, echoing the call of the Spirit to a
world lost without him:

> *The Spirit and the bride say, 'Come!' And let him who
> hears say, 'Come!' Whoever is thirsty, let him come; and
> whoever wishes, let him take the free gift of the water of
> life.*

Revelation 22:17

CONCLUSION

THREE DOORS

In this book, we have looked at the letters Jesus sent to the seven churches in Asia Minor. We've seen how the truth about those churches and the messages to those churches applies to us both individually and collectively in our time. In the last chapter, we saw how this results in a call for us to be whole-hearted in devotion to him.

But how do we do this? We saw as we examined the letter to Sardis that Jesus wants us to be human beings before we are human doings. But at the same time, we must recognize that the life of faith to which we are called will result in us doing something. So what exactly is that? Let's turn the page to chapter 4 of the Revelation to John to see what we can discover.

> *After this I looked, and there before me was a door standing open in heaven. And the voice I had first heard speaking to me like a trumpet said, "Come up here,*

*and I will show you what must take place after this."
At once I was in the Spirit, and there before me was a
throne in heaven with someone sitting on it. And the one
who sat there had the appearance of jasper and ruby. A
rainbow that shone like an emerald encircled the throne.
Surrounding the throne were twenty-four other thrones,
and seated on them were twenty-four elders. They were
dressed in white and had crowns of gold on their heads.
From the throne came flashes of lightning, rumblings and
peals of thunder. In front of the throne, seven lamps were
blazing. These are the seven spirits of God. Also in front
of the throne there was what looked like a sea of glass,
clear as crystal.*

Revelation 4:1-6

As John hears the words of Jesus to the churches, his perspective
is drawn upward to the heavens, and he sees an open door in
heaven. This is the door through which God speaks. A voice calls
John to enter the door, and when he does he encounters the glory,
majesty, splendor, and wonder of God himself.

The way John describes the splendor of this beauty is completely
overwhelmed by the symbolic language of apocalyptic literature.
In fact, John's description, as vibrant as it is, gives us just a
glimmer of the majesty John actually beheld as he looked to the
throne of glory. He also sees representatives of the Old and New
Testaments gathered before the throne, hears thunder and sees
lightning, and sees how the floor of heaven is the ceiling of the
world from which heaven can observe it.

John received an invitation to revelation, and countless Christians
over the years have benefited. But even more, it was an invitation
to a destination--the very throne of heaven.

*In the center, around the throne, were four living
creatures, and they were covered with eyes, in front and*

*in back. The first living creature was like a lion, the
second was like an ox, the third had a face like a man,
the fourth was like a flying eagle. Each of the four living
creatures had six wings and was covered with eyes all
around, even under its wings. Day and night they never
stop saying: "'Holy, holy, holy is the Lord God Almighty,'
who was, and is, and is to come."*

*Whenever the living creatures give glory, honor and
thanks to him who sits on the throne and who lives for
ever and ever, the twenty-four elders fall down before
him who sits on the throne and worship him who lives
for ever and ever. They lay their crowns before the throne
and say: "You are worthy, our Lord and God, to receive
glory and honor and power, for you created all things,
and by your will they were created and have their being."*

Revelation 4:6-11

When we enter the first door we are invited to, the door up, our
destination is a culture in worship in heaven. When we gather for
worship, and when we're stirred in worship, and when we sense
our spirits lifted in worship, we are actually getting a foretaste
of our destination. It's as though the door in heaven is standing
open, and we are invited to our destination. The invitation found
in worship reminds us of our destination, which is to be always
constantly immersed, saturated in the presence of God and to
worship him.

I don't know what that worship will look like on a day-to-day
basis in heaven. What we know for certain is that our destination
will be forever worship. So the first thing we attend to as we
think about what it is that Jesus wants us to do is the first door
mentioned here in revelation--the door upward, the door to
worship. Our first calling, our first priority, as followers of Jesus is
worshiping the Father.

WHAT IS WORSHIP?

The Scriptures are riven through with expressions of worship, and most of all Jesus the living word helps us to interpret the written word. And Jesus gives us the clearest definition of worship when speaking to the woman at the well.

Jesus was traveling from Jerusalem to Galilee, but instead of taking the route that most devout Jews would and skirting around the land of the Samaritans (which they considered unholy), Jesus led his disciples straight through. In the middle of the heat of the day, when they were tired from the journey, Jesus sent the disciples to get food from a village called Sika, and he sat down at Jacob's well. While he was there, a woman came to draw water. This was unusual, because normally women would come to the well in the cooler hours of morning or evening. But this woman came in the middle of day, and for good reason, because she was marginalized in her area because of her promiscuity.

Jesus spoke to this woman, which was also unusual, because she was not the same faith or ethnic origin as him. Jesus asked for a drink, and this request shocked her. She responded by saying that he was a Jew and she was a Samaritan. Jesus acknowledged this, and then demonstrated that he knew even more about her than she ever could have expected.

In this midst of this conversation, Jesus does two amazing things. He reveals unequivocally that he is the Messiah, something he rarely did in conversations elsewhere in Scripture. Then, while she asks him searching questions about what it means to be a devout follower of God, he describes to her what worship is all about.

> *"Woman," Jesus replied, "believe me, a time is coming when you will worship the Father neither on this mountain nor in Jerusalem. You Samaritans worship*

what you do not know; we worship what we do know,
for salvation is from the Jews. Yet a time is coming and
has now come when the true worshipers will worship the
Father in the Spirit and in truth, for they are the kind
of worshipers the Father seeks. God is spirit, and his
worshipers must worship in the Spirit and in truth."

John 4:21-24

I'm not very handy around the house. I can follow the
instructions for IKEA furniture, and I can paint and fix things
with screwdrivers, but I am neither an expert nor a joyful
handyman. In fact, if I try to get too handy, it tends to put me
and others nearby at risk. For example, back when I lived in
England, all the electricity in the homes is 220 volts, not like the
110 volts here. But I discovered that here in the States, washing
machines use 220. I discovered this because I couldn't get a three-
pin plug into the wall socket. So being the kind of handyman
I am, I tried to squeeze the prongs of the plug together. Then I
plugged in this "new-and-improved" cord into the outlet. As you
might expect, I got quite a jolt that day.

That kind of outsized power in a three-prong plug reminds us of
what Jesus describes when he says there are three components to
worship.

First, the thing that grounds us is that we worship the Father. We
worship the father not as a paternal figure, but as our Abba, to use
the intimate familial word Jesus used.

I was boarding a plane coming home from Israel on one of the
trips I've taken there over the year. On our journey back, a little
boy about the age of 4 sat in front of me. He was speaking a
combination of English and the local language. I assume it was
Hebrew, but it must have had elements of Aramaic woven in.
Throughout the flight, this little boy said things like, "Abba,

hold me." Abba was his way of talking to his daddy with love and closeness. This is the picture of worship. It's a worship of daddy, and an intimate connection with a Father who is deeply in love with us and wants to spend time with us.

Jesus then says that the worship the Father seeks is those who worship Abba in spirit and truth. Usually, when the word spirit is used in the New Testament, it has a capital 'S' and indicates the Holy Spirit. But on this occasion, all of the translators use a lowercase 's' for spirit. Jesus explains why this is. Because the Father is spirit (both Holy Spirit and small 's' spirit), those who worship him must worship him in spirit and truth. In other words, God's essence is spirit, and so we need to worship him from our essence. We might call this our identity. So Jesus is saying that true worship happens when we worship him in the intimate connection of Father and child, where the child recognizes his or her true identity.

Sometimes, to touch base with who we truly are, we have to go through layers of things that other people want us to be. We need to get down to that true connection so that we can cry, "Abba, Father."

As an Englishman, I was trained to have a thick upper lip and a stoic view of life. I'm not supposed to get overly excited about things (except for watching soccer, of course). Your cultural background may have similarly overlaid your true identity. What this meant for me was that my worship for a long time was stoic and stilted. It wasn't truly who I was, and it inhibited me from connecting with my Abba Father. God began to impress on me that worshipping him required more than I was currently giving, and a deeper part of my identity than I was prepared to expose. As I read the Scriptures and noticed the people who were truly and passionately in love with God used their entire bodies to worship. The Father was calling me to true worship that included a physical response to him.

Who we truly are needs to be covered by the truth. And of course Jesus is the truth. John's gospel tells us that Jesus is the way, the truth, and the life. Worshipping in truth means worshipping Jesus. So when Jesus tells the woman at the well to worship the Father in spirit and truth, he means that our worship must be covered by an understanding of who Jesus is.

WELCOME MAT

The first door we are invited to is the door of worship. The second door is the door in. Think back to the last letter to Laodicea. Jesus is standing at the door and knocking, and he says that if anyone hears his voice and welcomes in, he will inhabit their lives. Of course, Jesus is already present within us, but there is a difference between him being present and him being welcomed.

In Ephesians Paul uses the phrase "so that the Lord might dwell in you." He is indicating that we can go beyond the presence of the Lord being a truth to the Lord being a welcome presence in our lives. So how do we welcome Jesus into the various rooms of our lives?

Think about a room of fear and anxiety. Jesus stands at the door and knocks. If we open the door, we know from Scripture that perfect love drives out fear. Wherever you're afraid or anxious or worried, you can invite Jesus into the fear. Isn't that wonderful? We can invite Jesus who is perfect love into the room, and the fear will be removed by his love.

Think of a room of temptation. All of us are tempted. Jesus has been tempted in every way as we are too. Paul wrote the Galatians because they were disturbed and troubled by teachers leading them away from the good news of Jesus. He writes, "Walk by the spirit, and you will not gratify the desires of the sinful flesh (Gal. 5:16)" When you face temptation, invite the spirit in. Don't be ashamed .None of it surprises God. When I invite Jesus into my temptation, it's amazing how quickly the temptation departs. That's what the spirit of holiness does. So rather than being ashamed or condemning ourselves or thinking that we need to strengthen our will, invite Jesus in.

Now think about the room full of the challenges and difficulties of life. In John's first letter, he says, "He who is within you is greater than he who is in the world (1 John 4:4)." So as I encounter challenges that the king of this world puts in your life, you overcome them by inviting Jesus into it.

THE OPEN DOOR TO MISSION

We've talked about the door up into worship, and the door in that we invite Jesus to enter. Then there is the door out. Think back to the church in Philadelphia that had been locked out of the synagogue. Jesus told them that every door had been closed to them, he had closed, and that he had also placed an open door before them.

Philadelphia, like all seven churches addressed in Revelation, is thought to have been planted during Paul's time in Ephesus. Paul established the apostolic vocabulary for all these churches through his letters and his teaching, and Paul spoke about open doors as doors into mission. When he returned to his sending church in Antioch, he told them that there was a great door opened to faith among the Gentiles .Later, when he wrote from Ephesus to Corinth, he said that he planned to stay in Ephesus until Pentecost because a great door for effective work had been opened.

So when Jesus says he opened a door, he is inviting us to worship. He wants us to invite him into intimate relationship with him. And he wants us to go out. He wants us to understand that people around us may only have us as representatives of Jesus in their lives.

Do you know how often people go through an entire week without a word of kindness or mercy or encouragement in their lives? This isn't just true in times of quarantine and isolation, but in the everyday lives of many people. Going out in mission means going out in generosity in the spirit and the kindness and the mercy of God. As we do this, we will find opportunities to share our faith. We can take every opportunity to explain the hope that is within us.

The invitation is open, and the destination is clear. Which door is Jesus calling you to open now? The message to these seven churches, in whatever crises they are in, leads us to an invitation to open the door. No matter our crisis, Jesus is with us. So let us hear what the Spirit is saying to the churches, and respond by opening the doors to which Jesus invites us each and every day.